Find a Great Guy

Now and Forever

Find a Great Guy

Now and Forever

Kristin Kuhns Alexandre

Artwork by
Nicholas Papadakis

Runnymede
Press

Find a Great Guy: Now and Forever

Published by Runnymede Press

For further information, please contact:

Runnymede Press
P.O. Box 367
Far Hills, NJ 07931
www.thenewgentleman.com

Cover design by James Uttel

Artwork by Nicholas Papadakis

Book design:
ARBOR BOOKS, INC.
19 Spear Road, Suite 301
Ramsey, NJ 07446
www.arborbooks.com

Printed in Canada

Find a Great Guy: Now and Forever
Kristin Kuhns Alexandre

1. Title 2. Author 3. Relationships/Dating

Library of Congress Control Number: 2007943843

ISBN 10: 0-9776687-1-1
ISBN 13: 978-0-9776687-1-7

This book is dedicated to the men in my life.
It is dedicated to my father, who believed and trusted
that I would learn to make my own way.
It is dedicated to my husband, who is the love of my
life and who supports my dreams and hopes.
It is dedicated to my son, who I trust will make his own way.
And lastly—
It is dedicated to all the men I have loved and lost but
who nevertheless helped shape my belief system.

I want to thank my two children and my husband for putting up with me during the process of writing this book.

I would also like to thank:

All the men and women who helped me shape the opinions in this book through interviews and questionnaires; Diane O'Connell, who helped me weed through the good and not so good parts of this process; my illustrator Nick Papadakis; my editor and helpmates Dennis, Larry and Maria at Arbor Books.

TABLE OF CONTENTS

Find a Great Guy

Now and Forever

Her: "Darling, you're the best dancer."
Him: "Mmmm." (But thinking to himself: "I forgot to get that other woman's name and number.")

Lesson: Don't draw any quick conclusions about a man. He could very easily be a cad. This man is.

PART ONE
Introduction

Whether you're single, divorced or married, if you've pulled this book into your sights, you're looking for something. You're also wondering why it is that certain women end up snagging the good men.

In this book, a "great guy" is also referred to as Mr. Real Deal, as they are one and the same. Mr. Made Up is a man we girls create in our imaginations. This is the man we endow with wonderful assets that he usually does not have.

Smart girls know how to differentiate between a well-mannered man and a "great guy." What's the difference? That's easy.

A well-mannered man has been taught the rules and etiquette of a well-bred life. Nevertheless, he might still be a jerk. He may know to stand up and greet a lady when she approaches his table, but he could be thinking about how many beers he can down before passing out. He might bring two dozen roses on his first date but be wondering how he can get her to foot the bill for dinner. He might be nice to her Golden Retriever, then take her to a cockfight that weekend. He might clean out the car for her, then dump all his garbage in the town park.

A great guy might not know all the proper etiquette. It doesn't seem to matter, however, because he is interested in bettering himself at every opportunity. He is curious and open, and cares deeply for people. He asks genuine questions and seems connected. He's not defensive when asked about his life or his background, and he has nothing to hide. He's not as concerned about "things" and status as he is people and the world around him. His agenda is not to use people to move up the ladder—it is to do all he can to accomplish the goals he has set for himself.

The great guy has class, that is for sure. He knows his limitations and doesn't try to impress people. He stands up for what he believes in and apologizes if he goes too far.

My book gives hundreds of examples of classy men in situations where they prove themselves. A man with class is a man you can trust and believe in. His character shines through as he handles people and situations. He is not as rare as one might believe. He is a thoughtful man who has spent time thinking about himself, who he is and who he wants to be.

You cannot buy class. It is learned and developed; it is sought after. Men with class can cross boundaries. Take a look at Tiger Woods: He is a thinking man. Look at your man and the men you meet, then judge for yourself.

Rich girls hear about class from their mothers and fathers. They've been taught to avoid bars, men in fast cars and men who try too hard. They know all too well not to be impressed by big houses and show-offs. They've also been warned not to be impressed by inherited money. They know that "yesterday's trust funds" won't yield enough money to make today's young wife or mother satisfied for long. Their grandmothers told them not to marry for money, "or you'll earn every dollar of it."

All their lives, rich girls have been told that achievement and character are what matter. After that, they are warned that time is all-important—even more so than money, because you can't make more time.

When a man brags or flirts with other women, do what Grandmother said and "put on your running shoes and get out, dear." If he looks over your shoulder, you'll already be gone. Don't ever forget that the clock is ticking and you *are* special! Remember to always have something you love to do that you can make money off of. Keep your options open. Because if he turns out to be a dud, you may need an exit plan. Exit plans always remind men that you are special.

My book will teach you all of these things and more, and provide the best approach to finding a great guy. I will also share some wonderful information about the history of the gentleman and a bonus chapter on how to raise a gentleman.

It is my intent to open your eyes to the opportunities you have in front of you every day. You may already be dating or even living with your very own Mr. Real Deal. You may not know it, but your upbringing or unrealistic expectations may be keeping you from finding the man you need.

Please be advised that the information I am sharing with you took me three husbands and Lord knows how many failed relationships to learn and master. I was one of those rich girls, yet I did not have the right tools to find a partner for myself.

My own mother, herself an orphan, could not pass down the information I needed to find him.

So what does it take to avoid the perils of meeting, dating and marrying questionable men?

It takes knowing what you're looking for (hint: a man who answers questions and is reliable and honest). It takes trusting your instincts, and knowing when to get out when a man becomes evasive or resistant to getting close or answering simple questions.

It isn't easy to find a great guy.

Somehow, it seems harder to find a good man than a good woman, especially in America. Capitalism has a dominant theme and a major flaw: It's all about making money. Make money, guys, and the girls will come flocking to your door! The problem here is that desirable traits like kindness, attention to child-rearing, love of nature and enjoyment of life are all put aside for the dominant goal of making money.

Once we appreciate that men have a hard time living within our culture, we can better understand how to approach them. Men are more like us women than we think. They are trying to make do, survive and gain respect, just as women are. They wake up in the morning, grab their cell phones and walk around in their little bubbles, wondering whom to connect with, ignoring their surroundings and thinking, *Who should I call next?*

Yep, they're just like us. Their biggest fear is that there will be nobody to call. Their next biggest fear is that they will not have enough money to keep body and soul together, and if they do not have enough money or the ability to make enough money, then they will not be able to take care of their families.

If they are single, they will have no one to speed-dial, and nobody will speed-dial them, either.

So, why this book?

It is my firm belief that there is an untapped group of men in America—the rich haven't grabbed them all yet—and I intend to let you in on their secrets. I intend to level the playing field.

I believe I can help you, and the generations of women who follow you, find your own great guy—your own Mr. Real Deal.

Her: "This place is sensational. I love being here in the wild with you."
Him: "This is just the best!"

Lesson: A real Great Guy appreciates nature and all it has to offer.

CHAPTER ONE

SINGLE AND SEARCHING

Open Your Eyes—Open Your Mind!

The man of your dreams *is* out there. He's out there thriving and in abundance. You just need to figure out how to get him to stand up and be counted. We have to recognize him for who he really is, and although this might be tough, as we are all taught to look at the obvious "stars". Our parents have always taught us to look at the track or football or even tennis champs. "Why not see what he's up to?" It can often be very easy to overlook Mr. Real Deal who may not be so obvious.

Mr. Real Deal might be, in a sense, dressed in camouflage. He might not be featured in the school or local papers like other winners.

Later on in life he might be sitting in the boardroom of a major corporation or in a classroom filled with second-graders. He could very well be a master of three languages or speak very little English at all. The guy we're talking about might take a bus to work or drive a Mercedes, but that's not what defines him. Don't let something like that define him in your eyes either. He might earn an hourly wage pounding nails or a small fortune trading stocks; I'd also warn you against using that as a measure of the man.

What am I talking about?

I'm talking about a man who might have been left behind during the Roaring '90s, when the stock market took off and the Internet and cell phones took over. The man I speak of might even be a geek and keep his phone connected to his belt. He might work with his hands instead of with his computer. The man I speak of might work outside where he'll be aware of the Earth. He might be a builder or painter or plumber.

Let's take a hard, long look at men who work outside the office place. These are the men who might run or own your local deli or pizza shop.

This fellow will be involved in his community. He has to get along with people and please people. Now look around yourself and wonder:

Who runs and owns that car wash?

Who runs the local coffee shop?

Who runs the parking lot, the dry cleaners and the yard service company? These individuals live to serve, and must, by necessity, get along with people.

If you are divorced and single, take a long, hard look at the people who work at your daughter or son's schools. The teachers who care for your children are people who have put aside capitalistic dreams and who care more about self-fulfillment. If these men lived in Japan, they would be paid top dollar.

But in our country, teaching plays second fiddle to running a hedge fund or a company. Remember, money will not be everything in the long run. Do not sell out to all the capitalistic propaganda you are handed. Open your eyes and your imagination and start breaking into conversations with some of the men around you. You might be amazed at the men you have ignored or written off. Every grocery store, every gas station, every park is the product of someone's imagination or dream. It is your job to put down your cell phone and get out there and be involved with your world.

Remember: Time Can Do So Much!

Recently, I missed a high school reunion in my hometown of Dayton, Ohio. I always recommend attending reunions because they expand your horizons. They also shake up your premeditated images of people. If Jake was a loser in the eighth grade, how did he make out over the last 30 years? But when I had to miss my reunion, I asked the coordinator to have all the e-mail addresses and information passed on to me.

In most cases, the people I thought were winners did turn out to be winners in the long run. But there were some very interesting exceptions. These classmates turned out to have really amazing lives—and I never would have thought it.

One classmate, a girlfriend, ended up marrying a scholar and scientist. Her husband has found fame in an unusual niche all his own—bird songs. He has written several fascinating books on bird songs and has traveled by bike all around the world, in some cases biking with their son, a Stanford University graduate and also a scientist. Their son is currently biking thousands of miles, sponsored by people and organizations against global warming.

Chance Meeting

My girlfriend had just finished college when she went home to get a part-time job. She had to take some tax forms over to her parents' accountant one afternoon. As she walked in, a handsome young man approached her. "May I help you?" he asked. "Yes," she replied in a great big hurry. "I've got to drop off my parents' tax returns here and then get going."

"Why don't you slow down and let me take you out to lunch first?" he offered. This young man might not have married my friend later if she had been in more of a hurry. As it turned out, she came to her senses quickly and did not pass up a golden opportunity.

Carol was on the island of Nantucket ten years ago when she saw a "For Sale" sign posted on a very sweet-looking used Jeep. She called the number on the car and ended up taking a test drive with the owner. "He told me his family was in the automobile business and that he worked at a local boatyard. Normally, I would not have given someone who seemed blue-collar a second look. But this man was so kind." Carol is now married to her "blue-collar" man, and they just sold his boatyard to a corporation that is planning to build a private club. "We have an amazing life," Carol says. "Thank God I called about that car."

How do you know if a blue-collar man is above board or even available?

When you meet someone new and strike up a conversation, make sure you ask a lot of questions. Do not be shy. These questions are the key to everything that follows. If a man resists and feels you are being too pushy, beware. There is a reason he will not or cannot answer. And never forget that the best time to find out information is at the start of a relationship, not in the middle or, God forbid, at the end.

Men like to share their "story" in the beginning and, like all of us, will become more tentative as they have more invested, hence, more to lose. Let me give you some examples of what I mean.

After you've been seeing someone for a while, he will be reluctant to tell you he got beaten as a child, or was made fun of by classmates as an adolescent. You don't believe me? Then do your own trial run. I know it seems odd, but it is the total truth. Men will share so much in the beginning of a relationship, if you just ask. Ask him who he was dating. Why did it end and how? Are they still friends or does he harbor bad feelings? What went wrong?

Never forget that all of us have patterns. We all look for people who remind us of something. Most men will take you to the same places they took their girlfriend. They will give you the same sort of gifts they gave her. If they are nice to you, they will have been nice to her, too. I know you want to feel different, but trust me, men repeat themselves, over and over and over. If they were unfaithful to her, they will be unfaithful to you. If they are critical of you, they were of her, too. Sorry, but it's the truth.

One friend of mine was seeing a man who was the head of a huge soft-drink company. A group of us girls were having lunch one day when my friend shared her pleasure in receiving a huge crate of soft drinks, hand-delivered to her apartment door. "He was so sweet," she said, sharing her obvious delight in the gift. "Oh, he sent me the same box of soft drinks when I was seeing him," another girlfriend said. "He always has an employee run that stuff over to a new girl's house."

So much for that guy. He was toast. And he probably meant well.

There's a great scene in *Sex and The City* when one of the characters takes her lover's former wife to lunch. Suddenly she must confront the truth from a woman who learned the hard way that this was a very selfish man. I believe that a woman should truly do her research.

A friend of mine went on a Web site and joined up to meet single men in our area. Recently, she dated one of the men she met online. "He told me he couldn't give out his phone number or address because he had done this before and ended up being stalked."

I expressed my surprise that my friend's probing had not gone further. "Did you ask the man why he continued to date strangers he'd met online when he'd had such a bad experience?" The stalker story seemed odd and waved all sorts of red flags.

My friend admitted that she should do more investigating

before going out with new (and potentially scary) men she'd met online.

It's always easy to look back in judgment on ourselves. Once you've made a bad decision and blown it, I recommend forgiving yourself and moving on. But remember to look the next man over more carefully. Hold your head up and remember that this is your life and your time we are talking about. Most of us care a great deal about the cars we drive and the trips we take and the restaurants we go to. We should just as carefully review the men we hang out with.

Lessons to Remember:

1) Ask questions when you first meet a new man. Do not be shy; realize you deserve to be surrounded by decent people. Be as careful as you would be in selecting a new car or house.
2) Worry less about how he feels about you and more about if you like him.
3) Take it for granted that he has habits and that you will probably be treated the same way he has treated other women.
4) This man could be a friend or something more important than a friend. He will have to earn it because you are important.

Her: "What a great guy you are for loving me and my pets!"
Him: "I love everything about you."

Lesson: Love me; love my pets. That's the way it should be. You want a man who is flexible and caring and who can put roles aside.

CHAPTER TWO
GREAT GUY OR CLASSIC JERK?

On the Right Track

Why Do We Call Him a "Great Guy"?

Because he's not defined by some old-school notions like age or occupation or a code of dress. Because he's not defined by some archaic definitions of class. So if that's what you've been looking for, it's not surprising that you may have gotten off on the wrong foot. It's simple, really.

The minute you run into a man who starts to single out

people by color or race (verbally or otherwise), I'd strongly suggest you not waste your time. This man is a classic jerk. The minute you bump into a man who is putting down other people to bolster his own ego, you've also run into a classic jerk.

Don't sell yourself short. The man you *are* looking for might be a senior in college, a senior citizen, or the senior member of his over-40 softball team. He might be a doctor of medicine or a Wall Street analyst, but he could just as easily be a kindergarten teacher or a grad-school student. Keep your eyes open.

You are looking for a man of passion because passionate men have and share interesting lives. You are NOT looking for a loudmouthed show-off, and sometimes the two men can be confused.

You'll know you're on the right track when you bump into a man who seems to be worried about mouthing off about politics or sharing his opinion. If the man you are talking to seems to weigh his words, that is a great start.

Desirable men of passion weigh their words carefully. Loudmouths weigh their words rarely.

Consider the Wisdom of the Ages

Here's something I think is worth keeping in mind. Remember what Confucius said: "The gentleman is calm and at ease. He calls attention to the good points in others while another man does just the reverse of this."

A great guy makes demands upon himself. You can spot this man by his energy and desires. He wakes up with a plan and has hope for his day.

A classic jerk makes demands upon others and relies on others.

If the man you are looking at seems rigid, watch out. He may be constrained by something that will invade your life if you connect with him. Nothing would be worse than to wake up every day with a man who limited your dreams and hopes. This is what happens to women in Third World countries. They are perceived as less than human and allowed no hopes, dreams or lives.

It would be fabulous to find a great guy who's as comfortable in today's high-energy world as he is sitting on the beach with his eyes closed.

He might be a pro at multitasking.

He might be a lover of nature living a more solitary life. In any case, it is the knowledge and the love of the pursuit that makes him special. He's defined by the moment he's living in right now. Picture that, and you're well on your way.

Don't write off a man who's a student of the past.

Look for someone with an eye on the future.

Look for someone who knows that his actions today reflect the past and have everything to do with what the future will look like.

Ask yourself this:

- Does he treasure life? That may sound silly, but it's not.
- Does he know that life is both precious and God-

given? Imagine what that means when it comes to how he treats you.

- Is he in awe of the gifts that nature bestows on us and is he willing to do what he can to protect those gifts? That's exactly the kind of great guy you want to take a walk in the park with.
- Does he view people with hope or despair? Think about that when you're considering a long-term relationship.
- Is he more interested in acting in the best interests of the group or trying to keep up with the guy with the Hummer in his garage?

> *"I do not feel obliged to believe that the same God who has endowed us with sense, reason, and intellect has intended us to forgo their use."*
>
> —Galileo

Chivalry Is Not Dead

Chivalry doesn't have anything to do with one gender being stronger than the other. It's called simple courtesy. It's called caring enough about your fellow human being to go out of your way to show it. You have a right to demand that of one another. You and I have a right to demand that of the men we're with.

Think about the following things:

Finances. Yes, they will matter.

Personal Relationships. What relationships has he fostered? Have they been healthy?

Spirituality or Ideology. Does he believe in God or a higher order and does that matter to you?

Ask yourself if the following questions are important when it comes to the man in your life:

Is he willing to take a hard, objective look at who he really is? If he's not, then it doesn't matter whether he's opening the car door for you or sending you flowers just for the heck of it.

Is he willing to take a hard, objective look at what he truly has in his life at any given moment? He doesn't have to be totally content with what he has, but you don't want someone who's obsessed with what he *doesn't* have.

Is he living in the past? If so, there's not much chance you're going to change that. Holding on to the past is a deadend street. It takes away from his ability to make the most of today and to plan for tomorrow. Life is a roller coaster. But despite the inevitable ups and downs, you want a partner who sees it as a worthwhile ride.

Let's be fair. We all have disappointments and regrets and setbacks. We're not going to find a man who doesn't. What sets a great guy apart from the classic jerk is his willingness to learn what he can from those bumps in the road and then put them aside. What makes him different is a willingness to look openly at his own situation and the state of the world around him and move forward.

If you find a man like that, hold on to him.

Jumping in With Both Feet

Longing for yesterday is a waste of time and energy. A positive future isn't built that way.

Jumping into today with both feet is the only way we can make a difference in the world. If you want to meet a man who thinks the same way, get involved.

Find some place to put your energy.

Volunteer.

Teach.

Reach out.

That's exactly what a man who has his life together will be doing.

How to Find Someone Like You

Go onto Google and type in the key words that mean something important to you:

"Poetry"

"Dogs, cats"

"Environmental groups"

"Save the world"

It will not be long until you will find people with similar interests. A man who shares your interests might provide comfort, but I will make no promises.

I once married a man who shared many of my interests and we are now divorced. One of his interests did not turn out to be pleasing me in any way.

WARNING! WARNING! Shared interests are less important than shared values.

So what are shared values?

Shared values are things like how a man treats people, how he treats his commitments, and how he feels about life in general.

Does he feel life is out to get him?

Does he feel life is an uphill battle and that he has been mistreated?

Again, ask questions and then ask more questions. If he could write his own epitaph, how would it read? Sound morose? It's not as bad as a really bad breakup.

Crisis Management

Every day we deal with issues that threaten our very way of life. And while some enjoy an abundance of wealth and prosperity, too many others are faced with such life-threatening events as mass starvation, the ravages of AIDS and the threat of tyranny.

We never know when and where the next crisis will strike. It could be of the same terrible magnitude as 9/11, or a recession that strips away part of your retirement. It could be a global crisis or one that finds a community fighting for its survival.

It doesn't matter. A crisis is a crisis. It's no wonder we want to surround ourselves with men we can trust. It's no wonder we want to associate with men with values like honor, integrity and respect. Men who value action. Men who are flexible and strong and willing to step up to the plate when times get tough.

"A gentleman is a man who is clean inside and outside, who never looks up to the rich or down to the poor, who can lose without whimpering, who can win without bragging, who is considerate of all women, children and elderly people, and those who are weaker or less fortunate than he is. A gentleman thinks of his neighbor before he thinks of himself and asks only to share equally with all people the blessings which God has showered upon us."

—Charles Wiggins II

A Man Among Men

Isn't that the ideal of what we're all looking for? We want a man who sets himself apart by his bravery, curiosity or even thoughtfulness.

Recently I read about a small cruise ship that set sail out of Miami. When some unwelcome pirates attempted to board the ship and shot grenades and machine guns, the unbelievable took place. A cool, level-headed captain powered the ship up and out of the pirates' reach. Also onboard this ship was a passenger with enough courage and foresight to capture the faces of the pirates on his camera.

I know that when I revisit the turmoil of 9/11 and see a New York City fireman climbing desperately *toward* the disaster, up the steps of those collapsing buildings and straight into the arms of his own demise, I understand the true meaning of heroism.

When I hear about men who were trapped in those towers, cell phones in hand, calmly telling their loved ones what to do with their life insurance policies, I recognize the essence of courage and conviction. When I hear about them leaving messages for their wives and families and putting the welfare and peace of mind of others above their own, I glimpse the core meaning of love.

Her: "What are you doing? I love that you're taking over not just my apron—but my kitchen."

Him: "This is what I like to do—make you happy."

Lesson: Mr. Real Deal is secure enough and flexible enough to change roles and make it seem simple and pleasurable. Keep him in your house.

CHAPTER THREE

THE RIGHT STUFF: DOES YOUR MAN HAVE IT?

Take a close look at the man you're dating. If you're only in the yearning stage, take a close look at the fellow you're hoping to date.

Picture the man of your dreams. Take a moment and breathe life into him.

Now let's talk about the qualities we're hoping to see there.

Don't expect perfection. But don't settle for less than what you deserve, either. Whoever said "life's too short" wasn't kidding. Let's make it worth your while.

❧ ❧ ❧

Quality #1: A great guy possesses an inner calm.

This is something you should be able to sense. You can see it in the way he holds your eye. It's the way he makes you feel comfortable, no matter what the circumstances.

Here is a man who seems to be at peace with the world. He is at ease with himself. He tries to find the best in people. He's got enough confidence in himself to know he can make a difference.

He sees the big picture. He's also humble enough to know that the world will keep on going long after he's gone.

Lessons to Remember:

1) Listen to the tone of his voice; if you sense something defensive or cynical, you might be better off with a good book.
2) Bragging or boasting are sure signs of insecurity, and an insecure partner may be more than you want to "tackle."
3) Check out his posture. A guy who slouches might only be in need of some good, old-fashioned prompting. Then again, he might also be looking for a girl to prop him up, and you should ask yourself whether that's the kind of part-time work you're looking for.

When You're Looking for Ideas, Picture the Ideal

Picture the self-possessed and joyous face of the Dalai Lama when you're looking for a far-reaching example of a man blessed with inner calm. There are, I assure you, aspects of the Dalai Lama in every great guy I've run into.

Young adults are drawn to the Dalai Lama by the thousands. Why?

Is it his infectious giggle and playful smile?

Is it his wisdom and sound thinking?

He seems to have the answers to so many of life's questions, yet there is an element of simplicity in his message.

How would the man in your life react if he heard the Dalai Lama say, "Take into account that great love and great achievements involve great risk?" How would you want him to react?

The Dalai Lama says, "Remember that the best relationship is one in which your love for each other exceeds your need for each other."

Would your man get it?

Would he be inspired?

Would this resemble any relationship you have ever had?

"To be nobody but yourself in a world which is doing its best, night and day, to make you into someone else means to fight the hardest battle which any human being can fight; and never stop fighting."

—e. e. cummings

Quality #2: A great guy makes the most of life.

Look for a man who genuinely appreciates what he's got and chances are, he'll appreciate you as well.

Look for a man who knows when to count his blessings, because a guy who does also knows that his own good luck can change in a heartbeat.

You want a man who's adopted the attitude that life's worth living no matter what he might encounter. The man you want tempers his expectations of others, but never of himself. He likes to laugh, but a few minutes of silence are fine, too. If sickness or bad luck takes him by surprise, he calmly appraises the situation and seems to adapt to his new circumstances.

Lessons to Remember:

1) It's nice to be with a man who appreciates life and how precious it is.
2) A problem solver isn't afraid to make a mistake. He doesn't look for someone to blame. He fixes the problem and moves on.
3) Optimism is catching. Bitterness is contagious. Neither is a condition you're likely to change.

You might think that if anyone had the right to be bitter, it would have been Christopher Reeve, a man whose life was irreversibly changed by a tragic fall from a horse. Rather than fall victim to bitterness, he chose optimism. While confined to a wheelchair, Reeve still shared in the joy of his growing children. He traveled the globe raising money for others with spinal cord injuries and speaking his mind. No one ever told Reeve he would not walk again. Many doctors believed he might.

How a man responds to adversity is important. How he handles his own misfortune is a definite indicator of how he will respond to someone else's, including yours.

> *"Let us endeavor to live that when we come to die even the undertaker will be sorry."*
>
> —Mark Twain

Quality #3: A great guy does not rush to judgment.

The last thing you or I want in our lives is a man who stands in judgment of everything we do and say. Worse yet is a man who criticizes the way other people live, what they believe in, or the things they value. This shows a lack of respect and a lack of confidence, and the great guy lacks neither.

You want a man who's generous with his praise.

You want a man who's tolerant and patient and not afraid to make a mistake.

Sure, that's a tall order, but why not go for it?

Lessons to Remember:

1) You want a man who relishes diversity; without it, you can bet that life is going to be dull and boring.
2) It's not what the man in your life knows; it's what he's willing to learn.
3) Look for someone with the courage to speak out in the face of injustice. Look for a man who is willing to stand alone when his ideas are challenged.

A Great Role Model for the Ages

Most of the world recognizes that Jesus Christ was a man of uncommon valor. He set the highest standard for tolerance, and he refused to judge people based on their beliefs or differences. That's exactly what we're talking about as an ideal.

Jesus valued love and compassion above all else, and it's hard to do better than that.

Still, Jesus was a man. He suffered. When his friends betrayed him, it hurt. Yet, he understood their actions and forgave their betrayals. When his detractors sentenced him to death, he forgave them as well.

If that seems extreme, then take it down a notch. The last thing you want in your life is a man who holds a grudge; you want someone who knows how to forgive and forget.

> *"If you judge someone, you have no time to love them."*
>
> —Mother Teresa

Quality #4: A great guy takes a passionate interest in the world around him.

A great guy will be the man who thinks about the small things, like picking up a piece of trash in the park or sharing a smile with his neighbor. He uses his relationships with other people as a measuring stick of his success.

He's the kind of man who isn't afraid to take an unpopular political stance or stand up for an injustice in your local community.

This is a man of passion. But, he's not selfish about his passions. He shares them with you, and he shares them with others.

Lessons to Remember:

1) There's nothing wrong with a guy making a big splash, but it's the simpler acts that most often impact other people.
2) A man who doesn't understand that his actions have consequences, and that he's responsible to the people his actions affect, is bound to cause you pain somewhere along the line. It's inevitable.
3) There's no way you can win with a man who keeps score. Instead, keep your eyes open for a guy who judges the success of his actions by the people he touches.

Meet Some Men Who Model What You Should Look For

Most of you have probably never heard of naturalist Galen Rowell. His zest for exploring the wilderness of our country was instilled in him by his parents. His respect for nature and the need to preserve it became a passion.

He took this passion and made it his life's work, turning to writing and photography and bringing his message of respect and appreciation for nature to a wider audience.

Find out where a man's passion lies. Test his enthusiasm for the small things, like a sunset or a perfectly grilled steak. Test his passion for big things, like kids or friends or family. Then ask yourself if it's a fit for you.

"95% of all success is just showing up."

—Unknown

Quality #5: A great guy is definitely not a "Me Generation" man.

The man you are looking for should demonstrate an interest in others; you'll know it when you see it because it's not something he can hide. Still, he's not out there trying to draw attention to himself; that's also something you can't miss.

It's nice when you meet a man who feels secure, someone who knows that his self-worth comes from inside. It's also nice when you meet a man bent on self-improvement.

Lessons to Remember:

1) No man is an island. Much of the happiness we'll know in our lives will be due in great measure to the relationships we forge with other people.
2) Keep your eyes open for a guy who's doing what he can to make the lives of his fellow men and women a little easier. He's not hard to spot.
3) It takes courage to stand up for a belief. What does the man in your life believe in? Is he willing to stand up for himself? Think about what that means to a long-term relationship.

More Model Men

The late George Plimpton, a man who quarterbacked for the Detroit Lions and went three rounds with light heavyweight champion Archie Moore, was anything but a "me first" kind of man. He looked at life as both an adventure and an opportunity to give back to others. As a sports journalist, he set his sights on discovering how other people felt about their lives, and his goal was to communicate those feelings through participation.

His first love, *The Paris Review*, is an ongoing publication dedicated to the advancement of young writers.

It seems like such a simple thing to reach out and lend a helping hand, but that's not always the case. A man who is self-absorbed and mainly interested in making his own life easier isn't going to go out of his way to make your relationship his top priority.

⁂

"Criticism is something you can avoid by saying nothing, doing nothing, and being nothing."
—African proverb

Quality #6: A great guy cares about the legacy he's passing down.

When I speak about a man's legacy, I'm referring to:

- People he's touched in a positive way.
- Ideals he's instilled in his kids.
- Achievements of the mind, heart and soul.

It's not a matter of acquisitions or things, though there's nothing wrong with a guy acquiring a few creature comforts. Did he make a difference in people's lives? Will he leave the world a better place?

If you want to know whether a man puts respect above possessions, just ask him. If you want to know if he's more interested in solutions than excuses, just listen to him.

Lessons to Remember:

1) If you're more impressed with the car he drives than the conversation he makes, then maybe you should ask yourself why.

2) If he views generosity in terms of dollars rather than warmth and love, ask yourself how this bodes for a long-term relationship.
3) Asking a man about his goals in life is a straightforward way to find out how he views his own legacy.

Listen to what American essayist Ralph Waldo Emerson had to say about successful living:

"A man is successful who has lived well, laughed often, and loved much; who has gained the respect of intelligent men and the love of children; who has filled his niche and accomplished his task; who leaves the world better than he found it, whether by a healthy garden, a perfect poem, or a rescued soul; who never lacked appreciation of the earth's beauty or failed to express that appreciation; who looked for the best in others and gave the best he had."

What do you think the man in your life would do if you asked him to define success?

Why not find out?

It might be a little heavy for a first date, but you often find out more about a man during your "first-date interview" than at any other time. I know I keep saying this, but it is true, and you should use it to your advantage.

"All know the way, but few actually walk it."
—Bodhidharma

Quality #7: The great guy believes in himself.

The truth is, we all spend far too much time worrying about

what our peers think about us. We want their acceptance and approval, and there's nothing wrong with that. It only becomes a problem when we allow that need for acceptance to go too far.

The men in our lives need to realize that for every action they take, there will be critics or naysayers telling them it cannot be done. We want to associate with men secure enough in their decisions and their beliefs to press forward.

Lessons to Remember:

1) Mistakes are part of life. Sometimes, they lead to even greater things. The man you deserve is hopefully smart enough not to make the same mistakes twice.
2) The man you want will choose the right path for himself. It may be a different path than what other men choose, but he'll know if it is right for him, and he'll go for it.
3) Asking advice is what smart men do. Forget about directions. All men hate asking for directions and that is different than asking for help in their lives.

Former president Jimmy Carter once described how demoralized he felt after leaving office. There were decisions he regretted. There were mistakes he had yet to repair. He was, nonetheless, still determined to do something to help the world, and he knew that if he truly wanted to make a difference, he had to think "outside the box."

After much thought and research, he created The Carter Center and put himself to work on behalf of Habitat for Humanity. This group has been hugely successful in engaging ordinary Americans in building homes for the poor, despite critics who assured them it would never work.

Here's the thing: We all have regrets. But when you find a man who's intent on optimism and action despite his mistakes, you'll know you've found a guy worth keeping.

❧ ❧ ❧

"Great spirits have always found violent opposition from mediocre minds."

—Albert Einstein

Quality #8: A great guy leads without dominating.

A great man understands that people begin to believe in themselves the moment they acknowledge their self-worth. Our guy is willing to give people the benefit of the doubt. He's not afraid of being wrong, and he's not shy about admitting it when he is wrong.

A leader like that brings these same skills home with him. He allows you to grow without getting in your way or feeling intimidated.

If a man feels a need to impose himself on every situation, he's not likely to change.

Lessons to Remember:

1) People begin to thrive when we take the time to recognize their value; don't settle for anything less from the men in your life.
2) A man who isn't willing to listen isn't willing to learn. He also has a respect issue. Beware.
3) Show him your trust. If he doesn't return it, find someone who will.

There is an old adage that says if you fail to trust people, they won't turn out to be trustworthy. If there is one man who understood this concept, it was Sir Edmund Hillary, the New Zealand climber who first scaled Mount Everest in 1953. Here was a man who recognized that such an accomplishment would be impossible without the men on his team. He also understood that their actions could mean the difference between life and death.

Sir Edmund's exploits might appear to take us to new heights of trust and reliance, but the fact is, there is no more vulnerable place than an intimate, primary relationship, and a lack of trust is a difficult hurdle to overcome. Be honest with yourself about even trying.

❧ ❧ ❧

> *"Our care should not be to have lived long as to have lived enough."*
>
> —Seneca

Quality #9: A great guy is a contributor.

Imagine a guy who instinctively knows where his talents can best serve.

Imagine a great guy who's learned the art of "pitching in," but who isn't out there seeking publicity or acclaim for his actions.

Picture a gentleman who appreciates that the most important thing we have in life is HOPE. He understands that there is an undeniable link between hope and planning—so long as there is hope, we can plan. Let me take it a step further: Even in the most hopeless of times, there is dignity.

Lessons to Remember:

1) Rewards come from making a difference.
2) Beware of the guy who complains about a lack of options.
3) The more focused a man is, the better his potential to succeed.

More Great Guys to Think About

As a child, Jonathan Jones' difficulties in school were conveniently labeled "learning disabilities." Alienated and often shunned, he turned to nature as a source of comfort and quickly discovered that in the great outdoors, no one was keeping score.

Recognizing the growing number of kids experiencing the same roadblocks, Mr. Jones now devotes himself to SOAR (Success Oriented Achievement Realized), an organization dedicated to building self-confidence while emphasizing problem solving and social skills. The idea is to focus on the talents of kids, not on their shortcomings.

We should all take Jonathan Jones' philosophy and apply it to our daily lives. Better yet, wouldn't it be great if we could find a man who was willing to do it with us?

"The best way you can predict your future is to create it."

—Stephen Covey

Quality #10: A great guy strives for achievement.

Beware of the man who is overly impressed with titles or gives too much weight to the various letters a person might have behind his or her name. If a man judges people based upon their professions, he probably lacks the depth of character that you deserve.

You're looking for a guy who recognizes achievement and strives for it on every level. He's a man who likes to work hard and who isn't afraid of a little sweat. He appreciates the satisfaction of a good day's work as much as he does his time away from the office.

Lessons to Remember:

1) The effort and commitment behind an achievement are what make it special.
2) Be enthusiastic about life and you'll attract a man who feels the same way.
3) Achievement isn't measured in the number of people patting you on the back or singing your praises; achievement is something you feel deep in your gut.

Some Famous Men Have Character Traits That You Can Admire

Martin Luther King, Jr. understood the true nature of achievement as well as any man. He once said, "We are prone to judge success by the index of our salaries or the size of our automobiles rather than by the quality of our service and our relationship to mankind."

King's ultimate dream was to impress upon America that all men are created equal.

Dreams don't have to be this earth-shaking, but it's wonderful if they are.

It's not so great when you are the one with dreams and your man doesn't want to share or even hear about them. You want to be in a relationship in which you can be all you desire to be.

In a recent interview, Oprah explained how it was a good thing that one of her serious romantic relationships broke apart. Her former boyfriend would often complain that she had too high an opinion of herself and her ideals. We are all thankful she did not listen to that man.

"Continuous effort—not strength or intelligence—is the key to unlocking our potential."

—Sir Winston Churchill

Quality #11: A great guy is an optimist.

We all want to spend our lives with a man who believes in possibilities. We want to go to bed at night with an individual who sees the good in people.

Put your man to the test.

Again, Ask These Hard Questions

Is he the kind of guy who believes that every situation has an upside?

Is he willing to seek that upside?

Is he content to sit back and let the chips fall where they may?

Is that the kind of attitude you'd want to take into a long-term relationship?

Lessons to Remember:

1) Optimism doesn't imply a "pie-in-the-sky" attitude. You want to spend time with an upbeat person.
2) When things go wrong, an optimist doesn't pack it in; he finds another way.
3) An optimistic attitude causes us all to act, not react.

Men Who Made the Best of It

Jesse Billauer was only 17 when *Surfer Magazine* hailed him as the "new man on the block." Among his fellow surfers, he was known for his fearless, spirited approach to the sport.

But a short time after Jesse's brush with fame, a surfing accident left him paralyzed from the waist down. Jesse didn't retreat to his bed. Instead, he decided to reach out to other young men and women with similar injuries by establishing the Life Rolls On Foundation, an organization dedicated to funding spinal cord research.

Good things happen when men and women stay positive. Optimism and discovery go hand in hand. We don't want to be dragged down by someone who sees a black hole around every corner.

> *"No pessimist ever discovered the secrets of the stars, or sailed to an uncharted land, or opened a new heaven to the human spirit."*
>
> —Helen Keller

❧ ❧ ❧

Quality #12: A great guy is a maker, a doer and a thinker.

It's no coincidence that a man who is humbled by his place in the universe is usually the first person to take an active role in our earth's survival.

So as long as we're looking for a significant other, let's look for one who works with nature, not against it.

A great guy is interested in getting the job done right, not just in the recognition that comes with it. He conducts himself with a sense of purpose. He creates change. He allows himself to be amazed.

Lessons to Remember:

1) There's something fishy about a guy who feels the need to justify his actions every time he turns around. I would highly recommend keeping your distance.
2) A man should let his achievements speak for themselves; the last thing we need in our lives is a guy who can't stop bragging about what he's done or whom he knows.
3) You're allowed to question a man's actions, but if you have to question his motives, trouble can't be far behind.

People Who Do Relevant Things

Pete Maysmith is a father, a husband, a law student and a marathon runner. During the day, he is the executive director of Colorado Common Cause. He is passionate and committed. For Pete, it's all about challenges. He says things like, "I think we can make a better society. I think we can make a better country. I think we can bring more justice to this world." When he says it, you believe him.

One way to judge a man's ambition is to measure his gusto for living. Does he set priorities? Does he follow his heart? Are you included in that picture? Are you going to be included in that picture?

"I am still learning. I always will be."

—Michelangelo

Her: (Thinking to herself) "This could be the man of my dreams."
Him: (Thinking to himself) "When we become an item, it will be goodbye forever to these miserable pets!"

Lesson: Make sure you know a man well before jumping into love. Remember that a man must EARN your love. This man has earned nothing.

CHAPTER FOUR

A HISTORY OF OUR SUBJECT

"Given the right circumstances, from no more than dreams, determination and the liberty to try, quite ordinary people consistently do extraordinary things."

—Dee Hock

The *Merriam-Webster Dictionary* defines a "gentleman" as "a man of noble or gentle birth…who combines gentle birth or rank with chivalrous qualities." There is an equally uninspiring definition that calls a gentleman "a man of independent means who does not engage in a menial occupation or in manual labor for gain."

I am obviously advocating that we put the *Merriam-Webster* definition away for good and look for the "greatest of gentlemen."

I think I know where to start. Let's take a step back in time and see how the concept of the gentleman evolved.

600 B.C.
Or, in Other Words, a Long, Long Time Ago

We begin with the legendary Lao Tzu, author of the even more legendary *Tao Te Ching* and father of Taoism. Lao left us with these words:

In living, choose your ground well.
In thought, stay deep in the heart.
In relationship, be generous.
In speaking, hold to the truth.
In leadership, be organized.
In work, do your best.
In actions, be timely.

IN THE WORDS OF CONFUCIUS
Or, in Other Words, Almost That Long Ago

Almost that far back, Confucius, the renowned Chinese philosopher who lived around 500 B.C. and way ahead of his time, used the term *chun-tzu.* The most common translation remains, "a man noble in virtue but not necessarily a noble in social status." Confucius, obviously a great gentleman himself, said, "If the gentleman is not serious, he will not be respected and his learning will not be on a firm foundation. He considers loyalty and faithfulness to be fundamental, and he has no friends who are not like him."

The key in Confucius' mind was **self-examination and self-improvement.**

A great gentleman is not worried about what others think of him, but is only concerned that he takes strides to make himself a better person.

Confucius said, "A gentleman is never distressed at the failure of others to recognize his merits; he is distressed by his own lack of capacity…A gentleman has reason to be distressed if he ends his days without making a reputation for himself."

In Confucius' view, there were three things that a gentleman had to guard against. Here's how he put it:

> **In his youth, when his physical powers are not yet settled, he guards against lust.**
>
> **In his prime, when his physical powers are full of vigor, he guards against strife.**
>
> **In old age, when his physical powers are decaying, he guards against avarice.**

Then he listed the gentleman's nine primary "cares":

> **In seeing he is careful to see clearly;**
>
> **In hearing he is careful to hear distinctly;**
>
> **In his looks he is careful to be kind;**
>
> **In his manner to be respectful;**
>
> **In his words to be sincere;**
>
> **In his work to be diligent.**
>
> **When in doubt he is careful to ask for information;**
>
> **When angry he has a care for the consequences;**
>
> **And when he sees a chance for gain he weighs carefully whether the pursuit would be right.**

Another timeless observation focused on "wise words versus good deeds." Listen to this. Confucius said "The gentleman prefers to be slow in word but diligent in action. A gentleman is ashamed to let his words outrun his deeds."

Furthermore, "A gentleman should be smart enough not to evaluate a man solely on his words, nor to reject a good idea because of who said it."

> **The gentleman sets his heart on virtue; the small man sets his on comfort.**
>
> **The gentleman thinks of giving support; the small man thinks of favors.**
>
> **The gentleman can see a question from all sides without bias; the small man is biased and can see a question only from one side.**
>
> **The gentleman understands what is right; the lesser man understands only profit.**
>
> **The demands that a gentleman makes are upon himself; those that a small man makes are upon others.**
>
> **The gentleman can influence those who are above him; the small man can only influence those who are below him.**
>
> **And finally, "The gentleman calls attention to the good points in others; the small man does just the reverse of this.**

"The gentleman," Confucius insisted, "is calm and at ease. He is dignified but not proud. A gentleman considers justice to be essential in everything."

Not bad stuff from a man who lived 2,500 years ago, in a time when most scores were settled by the sword and justice was claimed by the guy with the biggest army.

THE VICTORIAN AGE
A Huge Leap

Let's take a giant leap forward to the Victorian Era, that notorious time in the 19th century when prudishness and conventionality were in vogue. How was the gentleman viewed back then, and how does this Victorian viewpoint stack up against the likes of Confucius or Lao Tzu? Was our Victorian gentleman a figment of the imagination? Or was he truly every woman's knight in shining armor? Did he really exist then? And if so, what does he have to offer in our search for a great guy?

John Henry Newman, an English nobleman, theologian and author who lived during the Victorian age, defined a gentleman as "one who never inflicts pain. He is mainly occupied in removing the obstacles that hinder the free and unembarrassed action of those about him, and he concurs with their movements rather than takes the initiative himself. The true gentleman carefully avoids whatever may cause a jar or a jolt in the minds of those with whom he is cast; all clashing of opinion, or collision of feeling, all restraint, or suspicion, or gloom, or resentment; his great concern being to make every one at their ease and at home."

These are all very important standards which hold up in today's world.

Newman tells us that the Victorian gentleman is "tender towards the bashful, gentle towards the distant, and merciful towards the absurd; he guards against unseasonable allusions or topics which may irritate; he is seldom prominent in conversation, and never wearisome. He makes light of favors while he does them, and seems to be receiving when he is conferring."

There is something so appealing about that last line.

Newman says, "The gentleman never speaks of himself except when compelled, never defends himself by a mere retort, he has no ears for slander or gossip, is scrupulous in imputing motives to those who interfere with him, and interprets everything for the best."

Now we're getting somewhere.

Furthermore, our 19th-century gent is "never mean or little in his disputes, and he never takes unfair advantage. From a long-sighted prudence, he observes the maxim of the ancient sage, that we should ever conduct ourselves towards our enemy as if he were one day to be our friend."

Or in other words, never burn your bridges. There is no such thing as a "small enemy." That's about as good advice as you'll hear. How about these?

"A gentleman has too much good sense to be affronted by insults."

"He is too well employed to remember injuries." If that means he's too busy to sweat the small stuff and harbor grudges, then yes, by all means.

THE ROARING TWENTIES
Raising the Roof

Let's talk about a thoroughly challenging time in the history of great gentleman. We're referring to the 1920s, better known as the Roaring Twenties, the Jazz Age and the Age of the Lost Generation. Historians call it the decade of the greatest social change in American history.

If we were bouncing back from the disillusionment of the First World War, we were also rebelling against the shackles of the Victorian period. We Americans were abandoning these ancient ideas in favor of flappers, flaming youth, radio, movies, bathtub gin, the speakeasy and confession magazines. We were introduced to Freud and the "new" woman, cosmetics and blatant consumerism. From the ashes of war blossomed a wild and riotous age of big spending and bigger profits, an inexpensive car and more goodies.

There seemed to be more conflicts in the air than our gentlemen of days gone by had ever imagined, and some of them were dividing the good old U.S.A in a big way: There were those people in favor of alcohol squaring off against the prohibitionists; there were the city dwellers who began looking at their country cousins as lower-class citizens, who in turn began seeing our cities as dens of iniquity; there were Catholics against Protestants; there was the Ku Klux Klan fueling the blacks-versus-whites issue; and there was a rising rebellion against the open-door immigration policy that had gone on since the Civil War. There were also fundamentalists battling Darwin's evolutionists.

Put yourself in the shoes of a great gentleman bent on living by a set of standards forged in integrity, honesty and commitment to making the world a better place to be. It was a challenging, exciting time to live.

It was also a seminal time for women. We were stepping forward en masse and openly raising hell about our second-class status. The social patterns that had ruled our lives pretty much forever were being challenged. Women began smoking cigarettes and demanding the vote. What a shock to think that gender wasn't an acceptable reason for keeping someone down! The true gentlemen—not the cigar-smoking country club members or "keep 'em in the kitchen where they belong" crowd—recognized this rebellion, and many of them paid the price for their support.

The great guys of the time were faced with the challenge of balancing undeniable economic opportunity against the undeniable traps of money, me and more. Despite the prosperity, it was an easy time to find someone to prey upon or just plain hate.

Wow! It was a tough time for a gentleman. What better time to stand up and be noticed?

❧ ❧ ❧

REMEMBER THE SIXTIES
The Beatles, Bell Bottoms and a New Way of Thinking

Even if you didn't live through the 1960s personally, the stories are enough to raise your eyebrows and tinge your cheek with guilt. History has a way of doing that. Listen closely enough and you'll be forever left with the impression that the 1960s were synonymous with decadence, debauchery and a healthy dose of immorality. Listen closely enough and you'll hear about an era dominated by irresponsible youth, casual sex, mindless drug use and enough cults to keep everyone happy.

According to the stories, if you were a young man in those days, you didn't have to blink twice to find yourself in the throes of a wild orgy and the benefactor of every type of drug known to man. Women were burning their bras and demanding freedoms that even our friends in the Roaring Twenties would have found liberating.

Over time, of course, the stories have grown to larger-than-life proportions. The stories also have an unfortunate tendency to obscure a school of thought that the gentlemen of that era, as well as gentlemen of all ages, not only tapped into, but carried with them long after the Jefferson Airplane became the Jefferson Starship.

In many ways, the 60s represented a rather vibrant cultural movement, and behind that movement was a rather viable vision. You might call it a vision of human possibility. It was like this breath of fresh air reminding us that we could be a whole lot more than mere pieces in the vast social machinery made famous by the previous generation. The men and women of the World War II generation were driven by such things as discipline, duty, responsibility and sacrifice. These are virtues that allowed us to survive the Depression and the war. In the 60s, kids were looking for more, something richer and more beautiful and even more sacred. Why not go out and seek this inherent potential? Why not spend some time in self-discovery and creative expression? Why not learn just how much potential the human race has?

I'm not saying that this vision wasn't a convenient vehicle for self-indulgence and irresponsibility for some; it was. But the true gentleman of that era didn't miss the message. He embraced it.

And it's a message he continues to embrace today.

It's not to say that the great guys of that era didn't pass on a sense of discipline and duty. And it's not to say that he didn't teach his sons and daughters about the need for taking responsibility and the rewards of sacrifice. He did. But he did it with an eye on becoming an individual, not a cog in a wheel designed solely to push the status quo. To that I say, "Awesome!"

Her: "Stop! Please stop! You're scaring me and I want to get out now!"

Him: "Shut up. I'm going to kill this guy in front of me!"

Lesson: This should be the last date. This man's road rage indicates a problem that may not be curable.

CHAPTER FIVE

A BLAST FROM THE PAST

How They Did It Way Back When

In our search for an ever-expanding definition of a great guy, let's jump in our time machine and see what the days of yore can add to the equation. Not only have people throughout the centuries disagreed on the definition, but half the time, they haven't even been able to agree on who makes the grade.

PRIM AND PROPER

The southern gentleman seems to spark this debate more than most, and the famous Confederate, General Robert E. Lee, is a prime example. Lee's own definition of a gentleman is quoted more often than his surrender speech at Appomattox. While it's a bit of a mouthful, we should try it on for size anyway.

Lee says, "The forbearing use of power and the manner in which an individual enjoys certain advantages over others is the test of a true gentleman." In other words, power-tripping is out. This is one of those timeless concepts that separate the weak man from the man of character. It always has.

Lee then says, "The power which the strong have over the weak, the employer over the employed, the educated over the unlettered, the experienced over the confiding, even the clever over the silly—the forbearing or inoffensive use of all this power or authority, or a total abstinence from it when the case admits it, will show the gentleman in a plain light." What we hear Lee saying is that the man who finds it necessary to play a trump card just to play it isn't much of a man.

Then he caps it off: "The gentleman does not needlessly and unnecessarily remind an offender of a wrong he may have committed against him. He cannot only forgive, he can forget; and he strives for that nobleness of self and mildness of character which impart sufficient strength to let the past be but the past." This is easier said than done, even for a southern gentleman, but what counts is the effort.

Lee sums it up with this: "A true man of honor feels humbled himself when he cannot help humbling others."

In the 19th-century American South, lineage and pedigree were everything, though Lee didn't come right out and say that. He was the son of a Revolutionary War hero, and his wife was the great-granddaughter of First Lady Martha Washington. Decorum and honor, according to most of Lee's biographers, were characteristics he would never think of leaving home without. But the question remains, Was it genuine or was it for show?

When Lee met his longtime nemesis General Ulysses S. Grant for surrender at Appomattox, he wore a clean, crisp new uniform and polished boots, despite the fact that his entire army was in rags. Grant's own uniform was mud-stained and tattered. Not Lee's. Not ever.

GENTLEMAN ABE

Most of us know the remarkable story of Abraham Lincoln. His unlikely rise from a log cabin in Kentucky to the White House in Washington is what the American dream is all about. What most of us don't know is that this "stranger than fiction" odyssey produced a gentleman of uncommon principles.

As the story goes, Lincoln overcame a shiftless father with little or no ambition, a mother who died, then an adored stepmother soured by years of sharecropping and poverty. One biographer, Arthur Brooks Lapsley, calls it a "whole household squalid, cheerless, and utterly void of elevating inspirations."

Not a great beginning. Despite it all, Lincoln prospered. He grew up working hard. He supported his family doing everything from plowing fields and digging ditches to chopping wood and driving oxen. He was essentially self-educated. He read every book he could get his hands on; it was said that he would literally walk miles in search of new reading material.

By the time he was 17, according to Mr. Lapsley, "Lincoln had attained his full height, six feet four inches in his stockings, if he had any, and a terribly muscular clodhopper he was. But he was known never to use his extraordinary strength to the injury or humiliation of others; rather to do them a kindly turn, or to enforce justice and fair dealing between them."

This attitude prevailed once he entered politics and won a seat in the Illinois legislature when he declared "the institution of slavery to be founded on both injustice and bad policy." This took guts, especially at a time when an abolitionist was regarded as no better than a horse thief. But Lincoln refused to back down from his convictions, even if it meant standing alone. Now that sounds like a great guy in any day and age. Here's how Lincoln put it: "Whenever I hear anyone arguing for slavery, I feel a strong impulse to see it tried on him personally."

Theodore Roosevelt called our rail-splitting country lawyer "one of the shrewdest and most enlightened men of the world, and he had all the practical qualities which enable such a man to guide his countrymen."

It's hard to imagine that this president was almost not elected to office because the American public believed his poverty and lack of formal education would prevent the world from believing he was a "gentleman."

GENTLEMEN OF THE ROUND TABLE
What About the Legendary King Arthur?

Let's take a look at the code of chivalry that he handed down to his Knights of the Round Table as a way of conducting themselves, even if it did mean raising the sword once in a while, and see if the result is a man who could survive among our search for a great guy.

Arthur begins by telling his noble troops, "Live to serve

King and Country. Live to defend Crown and Country and all it holds dear. Live one's life so that it is worthy of respect and honor. Also, live for freedom, justice, and all that is good."

Hard to say about the King and Crown part of the equation, but the rest of it sounds good.

The celebrated Arthur goes on to say, "Never attack an unarmed foe. Never use a weapon on an opponent not equal to the attack. And never attack from behind." It sounds to me like Arthur would be disappointed by the current rules of war. Remember "shock and awe"?

"Avoid lying to your fellow man. Avoid cheating. And avoid torture." Difficult to think that the last of these is still relevant, but we've seen enough to know that it is.

Arthur insisted that a gentleman "administer justice, protect the innocent, and always exhibit self-control." He told his knights, "Show respect to authority, respect women, and exhibit courage in word and deed." Arthur expected a lot from himself and his men, just as you and I do.

"Never abandon a friend, ally, or noble cause; never betray a confidence or comrade, and always avoid deception." Arthur concludes, "Exhibit manners, be polite and attentive, and be always respectful of host, women, and honor."

I would say that Arthur not only meets the standard, he sets a standard worth striving for.

GO FLY A KITE!

It's hard to talk about the gentlemen of our past without returning to the birth of our nation and a man many people called the first American, Benjamin Franklin.

During his time, few Americans were more distinguished. Even fewer could match his achievements in politics, science and letters. His reputation was as renowned overseas as it was here in the United States. He made his home in Philadelphia and proceeded to become both a successful printer and influential writer. He founded Philadelphia's first lending library, first fire department and first post office. He served as a colonial regent in England from 1757 to 1762 and later helped draft both the Declaration of Independence and the Constitution. He even invented the swim flippers our kids still fight over in the pool. That's a lot for one lifetime.

Ben Franklin the man was influential enough to be called a model for the American character. Franklin was, in many ways, an eternal optimist; he never failed to see the bright side of a situation.

He prided himself on his sense of humor. He loved to laugh, and he recognized the value of laughter in times of trouble. He was practical, self-reliant, self-educated and completely unimpressed with wealth or titles. In many ways, he was the quintessential "great guy".

In other ways, as with former President Bill Clinton, people would say that Ben Franklin's indiscretions prevented him from earning the distinction of being called a gentleman. **Personally, I believe a man should be judged as a total package and not by his sexual escapades alone, but I'll leave judgment up to my readers, and the wives who loved these men.**

Franklin entered the work force at the age of 12, apprenticing in his brother's print shop until he turned 17. When Franklin left Boston for Philadelphia, he had exactly one dollar to his name. Here's a guy who ventured out into the world with little more than the shirt on his back and started a new life for himself. The one thing he never did was compromise himself. If he made a mistake, he set it right.

When Ben Franklin was a young man, he visited a "house of prostitution" and established a relationship with a woman who later gave birth to his son. Franklin set the record straight by taking the child into his home and making him a part of his family. I will mention here that Franklin's son did not return the favor. When Franklin became part of the independence movement, his son broke off his relationship with his father. He broke his father's heart and sided with the English monarchy.

From what we know of Franklin, he prided himself on two things: He always explored both sides of every issue simply because he never knew where the solution might lie, and he had what was called in those days "a strong sense of civic virtue," meaning he had a sincere desire to see improvement in the way his fellow man lived.

Sounds like the kind of man we could use in this day and age.

BULLY FOR YOU!

President Theodore Roosevelt once made this remarkable statement: "It is not the critic who counts, not the man who points out how the strong man stumbled or where the doer of deeds could have done them better. The credit belongs to the man who is actually in the arena; whose face is marred by dust and sweat and blood; who strives valiantly; who errs and comes up short again and again; who knows the great enthusiasms, the great devotions, and spends himself in a worthy cause; who, at the best, knows in the end the triumph of high achievement; and who, at worst, if he fails, at least fails while daring greatly, so that his place shall never be with those cold and timid souls who know neither victory nor defeat."

Could the pursuit of a great guy be summed up any better?

Roosevelt wore many hats. We all know him as our nation's 26th president. He was also a big game hunter and military genius. He pioneered the national park system. He built the Panama Canal. He won the Nobel Peace Prize. One biographer, David McCollough, described him as having packed "more into one life than any ten men of average metabolism."

Yet, when all was said and done, Roosevelt's greatest passion was his family. He once said that "having the happiest home life of any man" was infinitely more important to him than serving in the White House.

He went on to say, "The tasks connected with the home are the fundamental tasks of humanity. When home ties are loosened; when men and women cease to regard a worthy family life, with all its duties fully performed, and all its responsibilities lived up to, as the best life worth living; then evil days for the [nation] are at hand."

Roosevelt grew up in a remarkably close-knit family. His dad was, in young Teddy's eyes, "the ideal man." As a college student, he once wrote to his father, "I do not think there is a fellow in college who has a family that loves him as much as you all do me, and I am sure that there is no one who has a father who is also his best and most intimate friend as you are mine."

Roosevelt believed that raising young men and women "who valued love and respect" was the key to a better society and world. What greater lesson can there be than that?

"WHEN IN DOUBT, TELL THE TRUTH."

Mark Twain spoke these famous words. Interestingly, they were often attributed to Mark Twain the humorist, but in fact they spoke more directly to Mark Twain the gentleman, a great guy who was as forthright as he was honest and loyal.

Most of us think of Twain as the author of books such as *The Adventures of Tom Sawyer* and *The Adventures of Huckleberry Finn*, true American classics. And although the author didn't start wearing his famous white suit in public until 1906, just a few years before his death, for most of us, it is the most familiar image of this man. He is the cigar-smoking humorist and sage of a thousand quotes. The truth is Twain had a lot more going for him than that. He was a printer and a journalist; he worked as a steamboat pilot, a gold miner, a newspaper editor, an author and a publisher.

Twain prided himself on speaking the truth as he saw it. He believed in making a difference, and he knew he couldn't make a difference by standing on the sidelines. Sometimes it hurt his reputation. But Twain knew his reputation wouldn't mean a thing if it didn't reflect his beliefs. He once said, "Loyalty to petrified opinion never yet broke a chain or freed a human soul."

He was a devoted husband and family man. When asked what his definition of a gentleman was, he answered that a gentleman should "be courteous to others, faithful to friends, true to his God."

Of life, he said, "Let us endeavor to live that when we come to die even the undertaker will be sorry." This is a goal every man can endorse.

On the lighter side, he added, "The best way to cheer yourself up is to try to cheer somebody else up."

Her: "Oh, my gosh! You have really gone overboard!"

Him: "Oh, I'm just bringing a few things." (holding flowers, a gift and wine)

Lesson: Be wary of a man bearing too many gifts. Always remember that each gift should be followed by three personal questions from you.

CHAPTER SIX
WHERE ARE THESE GREAT GUYS, ANYWAY?

In the Blink of an Eye

You're dropping your eight-year-old off at soccer practice for the first time; she's nervous and so are you. The coach is there to greet her; he smiles and shakes her hand. Then he introduces himself to you. What is that warm confidence we hear in his voice?

It could be that the man is a creep or just used to being seductive. My suggestion is not to jump into anything with this man until further notice.

You're walking across campus on a snowy day. You slip and

fall and your books go flying. Suddenly, there's a hand helping you up and a reassuring voice; once he sees you're in one piece, he helps you retrieve your books. What is the calm assurance you see in his eyes?

There's a 50/50 Chance That This Is a Great Guy You Want to Meet

You're late for a doctor's appointment and driving like a crazy woman. By the time you find a place to park and rush into the office building, you're ready to turn around and go home. When you step into his office, the doctor greets you with a smile. In the blink of an eye, you feel better.

Don't believe for a second that this might be the man of your dreams. He could be a serial killer for all you know. Reserve judgment—please!!

You're in a nightclub with your friends. It's noisy and crowded. Most of the guys are too loud and too aggressive. Most of them are drunk or halfway there. He's not. You can see it in his eyes. His smile is confident. He gives you your space. Suddenly, the two of you are talking about art and politics as if you'd been dating for six months.

He could be a great guy or he could be a creep. Reserve judgment—please!

Look Around, Ladies

When there is a great guy in your midst, you can almost FEEL his presence. There's a sense of calm that's almost palpable. He looks you in the eye, not with that salacious leer that we've all seen a hundred times, but with genuine interest and as a matter of common courtesy. Think about that one distinguishable trait! I can't tell you how many men I've run into who couldn't hold my eye for more than a second. I'm sure you've all experienced the same. This could be a start. But that's all.

A man shouldn't have to force his way into your world. He should be willing to answer your questions and not make fun of you for asking. If he makes fun of you and your questions, he is NOT available. If he is not available, you do not want him. Period.

The minute that you sense RESISTANCE to your questions and to your inquiry, back off big time.

The Young and Old of It

Middle-aged men are generally the easiest to judge. They've had time to hone their skills.

Most of them have been subjected to do the most humbling of all tasks: raising children.

As parents, we are there to serve. Children don't give a hoot about status or rank; it doesn't matter if you're the president of a supermarket or the prime minister. They want their pacifier, their food and their bottle, and they want it *now.* Their needs have only one speed: urgent. It doesn't take more than a day of parenting to learn this lesson. This is the ultimate reality; it's gratifying beyond words, but it's also humbling.

Speaking from experience, I've found that you're more likely to find a middle-aged great guy in a bookstore, Home Depot or coffee shop than in a bar or nightclub.

Try a museum, a gallery opening or a fund-raiser. Try the tennis courts, the running track, or the health club.

If he's available, he won't try to hide it. Look for the signs. An admiring glance is nice; eye contact is even better. If there's a ring on his finger, take the admiring glance as a compliment and move on. If there's not, well then, a word of encouragement might not be out of order. But always be on guard and full of questions when you are meeting a new man.

From now on you want only quality people in your life.

"I put more stock in a man's ability to carry on a coherent conversation than the date on his birth certificate."
—Jessie, a 27-year-old model and M.B.A candidate

Younger men need to be judged more slowly. They are more impulsive and less experienced in the ways of the world, and becoming a great guy takes some practice. Give them time.

Here are some things to look for:

A great-guy-in-the-works is generally open to suggestions about life. He won't be a know-it-all sort of guy. He's a sponge for new information and a willing student, and he has the depth of character to realize that he stands to learn much from others. He listens. An insecure man will shut you out immediately for fear that you will find him out.

Now, in general, insecure men can be a problem. However, since we all have our own insecurities, we should not judge too quickly or too harshly. A young man might become confident later in life, as he finds his way, so it's up to you to judge carefully.

Keep This in Mind, Too

Young great guys have generally been taught to plan ahead; you can see it in their behavior. They're self-sufficient, but they're not shy about asking for help, either. They're the ones with the sense of adventure and the wealth of optimism.

You might find this guy sitting with his friends at the local coffee shop, but you won't find him criticizing the government or bad-mouthing some institution without offering solutions on the flip side.

His sense of optimism won't waiver just because he hasn't been blessed with an abundance of good fortune or economic success. He's a positive thinker; you can hear it in his conversation. He never feels cheated, especially around you.

He's the kind of guy who believes we can design our lives any way we choose.

Speaking From Experience

I've found that you have a better chance of spotting a great guy on the ski slopes or on a mountain trail than in singles bars, although having a beer with the boys is not off limits. I also prefer meeting people while in action. Try going to a golf range or bowling alley, or joining one of those large, outdoor tennis clinics.

And yes, in this day and age, you might even find him on the Web. Though I'm not altogether sold on the online dating services and matchmakers promising you your future mate, I won't necessarily avoid them, either. I've done crazier things than that; we probably all have. Go for it. See what's out there.

However... DO NOT EVER reveal your street address to anyone on the Web. You've heard all the horror stories and you know all too well that anybody can embellish themselves very cleverly on the Web and hide behind a screen name. Do not ever meet anyone you encounter on the Web in a place that is not VERY PUBLIC.

"No man is worth your tears and the one that is won't make you cry."

—Brian Littrell, singer, songwriter and philosopher

Driver Beware: Women Are Watching You

Does he pull over if someone is tailgating him?

Does he have a heavy foot?

Is he the kind of guy who'll stop and help a driver in distress?

Is he willing to give up his keys after a couple of cocktails?

Is he the kind of guy who insists he's fine when it's clear he's not?

There are a hundred examples just like these, and every one of them opens a window on a man's true persona. And since there's hardly a man on the planet that doesn't drive, you are in luck.

You be the judge.

Do you want to hook up with a man who seems willing to risk his life and yours by ignoring the law? That's exactly what he's doing if he's driving drunk. And that's exactly what he's doing if he's tailgating. What does that say about his state of mind? How much respect is he showing for himself, for you, for the other people on the road? How would you feel if your children were in the car with this man? I'm pretty sure your answer and mine would be the same.

❧ ❧ ❧

Ask Yourself These Questions

Is his car a garbage pit? If it is, it probably reflects a lack of personal pride, a generally chaotic state of mind, or a guy with more on his mind than making an impression on you or me.

Does he seem to care more about his car than he does about you? If he does, can you think of a better exit line?

Does he consider his car a status symbol or simply a means of transportation? A better question might be, Do *you* consider his car a status symbol or simply a means of transportation?

❧ ❧ ❧

"Don't compromise yourself. It's all you've got."

—Janis Joplin, singer extraordinaire

Ask and You Shall Receive

Great guys are everywhere.

One way to pursue the question of whether or not the man in your company is a great guy s to flat-out ask him. The great guys I've met over the years seem to know their status. They're comfortable being looked upon as gentlemen. It isn't a title or a status symbol; it's a way of life. They know they are great guys—because they strive to be gentlemen. It's who they want to be.

Other men also know they are NOT great guys. It's not in their repertoire. They simply don't want to be gentlemen, period.

What does it mean when certain men have no interest in being great guys?

Some men put no stock or importance in their behavior. An example would be Woody Allen. He will never apologize for having an affair or marrying the adopted daughter of his partner. His only regret is that he did not break up with his partner earlier. He couldn't care less about propriety or hurting people. He gives no importance to such stuff.

When we talk about FEELINGS, we talk about character. A great guy is a man who can feel your pain. He can put himself in the other guy's situation. And certain men are just not able to do that. Woody Allen has many amazing talents, but he cannot do what we are talking about here. Therefore, he is not a great guy or close to becoming Mr. Real Deal in any way. And I'm sure he couldn't care less about the label.

Don't be lulled into believing that a man is a great guy-based upon stereotypical traditions such as:

- Giving you flowers.
- Opening doors.
- Being polite to your family.
- Calling you night and day.
- Picking up the tab.

These are hardly conclusive proof of a man's integrity. Look a little deeper. Try separating your needs from your wants and trusting your instincts.

Patience Is a Virtue

Sure it takes time to determine if your man is a great guy. But it's well worth the wait.

Here's a sure-fire clue! Listen to the way he talks about his mother when she's not around; if he talks poorly of her, beware. Then listen to the way he talks to her when she is around; if he speaks unkindly to her, beware. Go a step further and ask him to describe the people he has loved over the years.

If you want a real relationship, make sure he does, too. None of us aspire to be a token girlfriend. Make sure he is genuinely interested in you, both as a person and as a woman. Make sure he has a genuine interest in women in general.

Here Is a Tricky Piece of Advice, But One Worth Mentioning

We should most certainly avoid men we suspect of being "in the margins," which is another way of describing a man who believes he is capable of having sexual relationships with both men and women. These are the kind of men who can erode our confidence and play havoc with any long-term aspirations we might have.

How can we uncover these "in the margin" men? Easy. Come right out and ask him if he believes men who engage in bisexual activities can be successful in having a long-term relationships. If he believes they can, beware.

Mr. Control Freak, a Real Problem Kind Of Guy

Then there's the controlling man. He's the man who calls a half dozen times a day because he "can't stop thinking about you."

At first, it seems exciting. At first, you're grateful for the interest. Then, it becomes an annoyance. When it starts to sound like he's checking up on you, you begin to feel uncomfortable.

Don't be surprised if he doesn't want you to expand your horizons or pursue your interests.

Why? Because doing so threatens his sense of control. When he feels threatened, he becomes a threat. He disguises his insecurity with criticism. He chips away at your self-esteem. If this doesn't work, he might become angry, violent or vindictive. He might chase other women to punish you. Under any circumstances, this is a man you need to get out of your life.

If you have any questions about the dangers of hanging out with controlling men, just consider the fate of a gorgeous California woman named Nicole Brown. She had two children with the famous football running back, O.J. "The Juice" Simpson. She was obviously awed when she first met him.

Nicole ended up dead in her front yard, her throat slashed, while her children slept in their beds. Her desperate 911 calls were played in the courtroom, documenting her former husband's frequent, violent visits to her house. Still, he got off. And he is now raising Nicole's children without her.

You ask, *What does all this have to do with controlling men?*

It has everything to do with them.

O.J. Simpson was a living, breathing example of a controlling man. He constantly told Nicole how fat she was, even when she was pregnant. He continually verbally abused her, telling her how stupid and unattractive she was. All the while, he was monitoring her whereabouts and cheating on her with other women as well.

How could Nicole have recognized right away that her man was controlling?

I suspect she knew right off the bat that O.J. was going to be a difficult man. There is no doubt that he exhibited possessive behaviors right away and was jealous beyond reason. The problem was that she allowed her heart and probably her ambition to get the better of her.

QUESTION! Do I believe Nicole could have avoided her untimely death by asking O.J. Simpson lots of questions early on?

Yes.

Had she not been blinded by his celebrity, Nicole might have spared herself hundreds of beatings from her own Mr. Control Freak.

⁂

> *"You live, you learn; you love, you learn; you laugh, you learn; you choose, you learn; you ask, you learn..."*
>
> —Alanis Morissette, singer, songwriter and woman of significant insight

⁂

All Things in Moderation

Carl Gustav Jung once said, "Every form of addiction is bad, whether the narcotic be alcohol or morphine or idealism."

People have always sought to escape reality or to reach some yet-to-be-explored "level" of consciousness through the ingestion of drugs or alcohol. The big question is whether or not the rule of moderation is observed. For the long haul, we all need and want a moderate man.

The fact is alcohol alters our personalities and changes our behavior, and almost always for the worse. Despite a myriad of ad campaigns to the contrary, alcohol does not make us more charming. And, sorry to say, it does not increase our sexual appeal either.

If the man in your life believes otherwise, he is not the guy for you.

It's a Matter of Moderation

We know there's nothing wrong with a man spending an evening with the boys at a sports bar or a nightclub. However, if the man in question fits our evolving profile of a great guy, it's a good bet he won't be the one getting loud and obnoxious after a few too many beers or making a fool of himself in front of a table of young women. You know the type.

Courtesy—which you and I have every right to expect—doesn't go out the door just because a guy's having a drink or two. And if it does, we have every right to expect an apology; a great guy wouldn't see it any other way. And, hopefully, he'd also wise enough to learn from his mistakes.

> *"You see a lot of smart guys with dumb women, but you hardly ever see a smart woman with a dumb guy."*
> —Erica Jong, author

Getting Things Done by Doing Nothing

Years of man-hunting have led me to the conclusion that a man can be either a follower, a leader or somewhere in between. So long as he is a decent man, it may not matter.

We live in a world where constant stimulation is the rule of thumb. There seems to be a constant and ever-present need for entertainment and distractions. Most everyone is a spectator. Few are players. Which are you? It's an important question to ask before setting out on the hunt for the ultimate great guy.

That's all well and good, but there's something that's equally important: It's the need to slow down every once in a while; it's the need to stop and spend some time with each other, with family and friends, with ourselves. If a man's not willing to grant himself that kind of time, he probably isn't going to be crazy about granting you that time.

A solid man enjoys his own company, which makes him that much better company for us. He knows there's a time and place for turning on the TV or cranking up the stereo, and he knows there's nothing wrong with wiling away a few hours reading a magazine or catching up with us on the telephone.

He's also discovered the value of a quiet walk in the woods or a stroll through the park.

"I do some of my best work as a person when I'm doing nothing at all. It took me a long time to learn that."
—Julia, 32-year-old realtor and biking enthusiast

The Powers of Observation

We women are usually considered the more blessed of the genders when it comes to the powers of observation, and I doubt any of us would argue with that claim. Still, we want the men in our lives to give us a run for our money in this area. We want someone who enjoys observing the world around him, someone who enjoys observing himself.

An open mind is as important as a quiet mind, so why not look for a man who understands this, too? Why not look for a man who knows that taking in a beautiful sunset is just as important as hearing his favorite band when they come to town?

Here are a few last thoughts.

Remember that a long-term relationship is going to be a relationship that involves your family and friends, and you want a man who enjoys their company. If you value their thoughts and opinions, then he should, too. That's not asking too much.

A great guy enjoys listening, and it's not about having his own views reaffirmed; it's about finding out something new. When he talks, people listen. You listen. Why? That's easy—he's not talking down to you or trying to be superior.

Her: "Beat you! Keep coming! It's fabulous up here! I thought you were a world-class rock climber and had no problems with the big ones."

Him: (Thinking to himself) "Guess I won't tell such big lies the next time."

Lesson: The more time you spend with a man, the more you will learn. Activities like golfing, climbing and hiking are great because you learn his real strengths and weaknesses.

CHAPTER SEVEN
MY OWN POINT OF VIEW

Like most women, I have made lots of mistakes in my own search for Mr. Real Deal. Like so many of us, I made life-altering decisions out of desperation rather than for the right reasons.

How can you tell if a decision you are making is desperate and this wrong?

It is not that hard to find the truth. For example, when you start comparing your situation to someone in your peer group, you are bordering on desperate. What do I mean? You say to yourself, "All my friends are married and leaving me behind.

I'm going to be the ONLY one not married or having children. I guess I should just go and marry John even though he is not what I really want."

Here's another example: "I am almost 30 and have no idea what I'm going to do with myself. I guess I should find a husband."

There are three things you should simply never do. I call these The Dreaded Nevers:

1. You are out there in the world worried about making it. You decide to find someone and marry him for money. You think this will solve your biggest problem.
2. You feel your biological clock ticking and decide to go out and find yourself a husband before it is too late.
3. You are 27 and still shacked up with mom and dad. This is getting old. You decide to get married to get out of the family house and get located in your own home.

Why are The Dreaded Nevers so dreaded? The answer is because they set you on the wrong path. In addition, your partner will have less respect for you when he discovers your reasons for choosing him. But there is something worse: you will have less respect for yourself. When you marry out of desperation, you will find yourself replaying your own thought process over and over again in your head, and you will feel badly about yourself over and over again.

What should you do when you genuinely feel desperate to change your life for the better? We all feel desperate at various stages in our lives. People who do not worry about "where they are" in life are either in denial or simply fooling themselves. All of us worry about milestones in life.

When you are 16 you start thinking about driving. At 21, you know it is legal to drink alcohol. At 65, people talk about retiring. But should they? Do you have to drink when it's legal or drive when it's legal or retire when people start talking about it? Of course not.

The fact is that we are all different and we are all on different clocks which just happen (for a very good reason) to be our own. If you feel that your peer group is getting ahead of you, it may be a good time to do what I call "a review" of your life plan.

Sit down with yourself and make some mental or real lists. Maybe you should start looking for a mate. Maybe it's time to get a real job or find a real home so that you'll be more appealing to a mate. Think things through. Think about yourself. Are you ready to pair up? Are you in good health?

Always start with the obvious: the obvious is your health. Are you taking care of yourself? Have you gotten a physical? Are you doing some sort of exercise three times a week?

Before you sell your car or your house, you generally give your car or house a complete once-over to check out probable value and condition. Okay, you are not a car or a house, but men will still be looking at you as someone they will be spending a lot of time with. If they can't tell right away how you are and how you take care of yourself, they are bound to do so later on.

You will want a partner who complements you. If you are an athlete who plays golf and tennis on a regular basis, you might want someone to share these interests with. If you are a biker or rock climber, the same holds true. If you love to read and go to movies, you will still want a partner who is healthy and who cares about his health.

So lets start with the obvious. Your health.

After making sure you are in good health, with a good exercise regimen, you approach a more difficult task. You review your state of mind. If you are feeling desperate, you need to analyze why.

This is not the right approach to finding the man of your dreams. You will need to be feel good about yourself before looking for Mr. Real Deal, who just might become Mr. Right.

How do you do that? I recommend getting involved with your work or helping other people. Calm down and give yourself a time frame within which to work.

Do some volunteer work for, say, three months, and then you might start a real campaign to look for Mr. Right, so long as you are feeling good about yourself.

How will you know that you are READY to go looking for a great guy? You will feel calm and happy about yourself. You will feel hopeful, and this is a feeling that completely replaces that feeling of desperation.

If you have reached this state, it doesn't matter where you look—you will have options. Doors will start to open. People will sense your goodwill and hopeful attitude.

I believe that there is more than one man in the world for you. There may be thousands of men who could share a wonderful life with you. You just need to be in the right frame of mind and avoid looking for something hopeless. What do I mean by that? I mean that Mr. Real Deal might pass you by without your even seeing him. You need to be alert. There are no thunderbolts out there. Real love takes time, and real affection and caring come from a foundation of trust and building a life together.

This is not Hollywood. This is better than Hollywood, because it is real, and you're the star of this show.

Her: "Come on. This is our sixth date. You can come in and stay awhile."

Him: "No, no. I don't want to push you. (Resisting completely) Let's go out somewhere."

Lesson: This man is resisting, and when a man resists, there is a reason. He could be gay or have herpes or WORSE. When a man resists your charms, stay away. He knows more than you do.

CHAPTER EIGHT

HOW TO RETOOL THE MAN YOU HAVE

You are already married or in love or very fond of the man in your life. But there are issues and problems, things about him that bug you. You wish with all your heart that you could change things about him. You'd just love him to be nicer, kinder, or more considerate of you and your feelings. You could certainly do with more of a great guy, that's for sure!

Can you change him? If he cares for you and your feelings and if he wishes to continue on with you, I believe he can change.

Change is about motivation and desire. So for change to take place, there must be a motivating force on his end. You must somehow show your man that if he becomes more considerate or more of "whatever you want him to become"—that it would be worth his while.

Allow him to understand that you will care for him more and be a better partner when the change occurs.

The way you bring about change is by very subtly and slowly pointing out people who possess qualities that you really do admire. For example, if your man is rude, you might say how you admire James Bond (the character in the films) because he is always so tactful and kind, even before killing his enemy.

There's a reason why advertising companies always repeat slogans and campaigns until you are sick to death of the rhyme or jingle. Repetition is everything. You must continue to reinforce how much you love men and actors and people in general who are kind and not rude.

The same holds true for any behavior you wish to change and correct in your man. If your man hates to bathe or brush his teeth, you need to point out how much you love it when he does. And you need to make sure you bathe and brush your own teeth often and in front of your man.

If your man raises his voice or speaks loudly in restaurants, you need to speak very quietly and point out how much you admire quiet and tactful men. If he does not have good cell phone etiquette, then you need to speak to him directly about it when he is off the cell phone.

If your man is overweight, you need to have a look at your own habits first. If both of you need to change your eating habits, you can undertake a project like this together. If he is overweight and you are not, you need to be careful not to be too critical, but to be supportive of his undertaking good health practices.

There's always a chance you will not be able to change your man. But you never know. Chances are he is not aware that what he is doing is bothering you or disrupting the relationship. And if he can change his behavior and better his relationship with you, why not try? In any event, you will never know until you try.

At one point in my first marriage, I realized there were things that absolutely had to change or I needed to leave the relationship. My husband had written a will and updated it and intentionally left me out. When I asked him why, he said it was because, as a lawyer, he knew that should he die, I would receive my fair share of his estate from the government. He said it didn't really matter what was in his will.

In protest I said that I did not care what the law said; I cared what he had put in writing. I felt that if I was not mentioned in his will, why should I be married to him?

I asked him to change his will.

He said no. That conversation began the process of ending our marriage, which was as it should have been. My husband did not have the nerve to tell me he didn't love me, but he did have the nerve to tell me he had just drafted a new will and left me (his wife of five years) out of it. That action alone says it all.

It takes energy and nerve to try to change something. If something about your man bothers you enough, go for it. If he loves you enough, he will make an effort to change.

If he doesn't, you may want to leave the relationship. You deserve the best you can have in a relationship, and so does he.

Her: "Last night was so much fun. You're obviously a sensitive man and you remind me somewhat of my father. Thank you for sharing your thoughts with me."

Him: "Sorry, I can't talk long right now. I have an architectural project due tomorrow, then I have to go out and run because I'm getting ready for the Philly marathon. I'll call you later."

Lesson: This woman has misjudged this man completely and endowed him with qualities he does not have. This is her Mr. Made Up. This loser will hurt her if she continues seeing him. In any event, he will waste her precious time.

CHAPTER NINE

STRAIGHT TALK

It's time now to introduce you to several men who I think fit the Mr. Real Deal profile in today's increasingly crazy and complex world. No, there are no kings or generals or presidents in this group. As we've already discovered, occupation and "station in life" are not musts in the making of a "solid" man.

Our group consists of a fireman, a doctor, a writer, a public school administrator and a judicial consultant. We have a contractor, a futures trader, a financial advisor, a schoolteacher, a forensic investigator and an actor. We talked to a pilot, a theater manager, a student, a gardener and a confirmed retiree. Their ages range from 19 to 81, yet age seems to have little relevance when it comes to character.

I asked them all the same questions. Their responses are based on my "For Men Only" questionnaire, and I invite all the men in your life to fill it out. As you will see, there is no right or wrong answer. These are men with definitive views on almost all aspects of life and with a handle on their place in the world.

❧ ❧ ❧

QUESTION ONE: Personal History. *Were good manners emphasized in your home? Other than your parents, who were the most influential people in teaching you good behavior?*

Going on the theory that experience is one of the great teachers, I began with Max, an 81-year-old retired great guy. He said, "Home is where it starts. All the schooling in the world can't make up for a lack of attentive parenting."

In his early 50s John G., a forensic investigator replied, "Good manners were absolutely expected at home. It was a matter of respect."

"Most importantly," said Bruce, futures trader, 54-year-old "my parents taught good manners through example. They treated their peers, their children and their friends with respect and dignity."

Though etiquette was something his parents emphasized in the home, Mark, a school administrator, "Good behavior was simply about being kind and respectful to others." A mentor in the professional world taught him the value of being "approachable," as well as making a priority of "the needs and attitudes of others."

Paul, a 25-year-old fireman, said that above and beyond his parents, "Good friends also had a positive influence on my behavior."

Steve, the writer in the group, made this observation: "My dad emphasized things like always looking someone directly in the eye. A firm handshake says more than any words. He'd say respect is earned."

"A defining moment came for me when I was riding a crowded bus to school one day," said Keith, a 19-year-old student. "I saw a poor, rough-looking man stand up and offer his seat to a woman as if it were the only appropriate thing to do. That has always stuck with me."

❧ ❧ ❧

QUESTION TWO: Self-image. *Please share the principles and values that are most important to you as a man. What sort of man do you see when you look in the mirror? What are you most proud of in your life? Being a good parent, a successful businessman, or a valuable community leader?*

In terms of his values, David, an Arizona physician, said simply, "Honesty, hard work and ethical behavior." He added, "When I look in the mirror, I see an ordinary man who is healthy and clear-eyed. Someone who loves his job and his family. I'm most proud of my accomplishments in setting goals throughout my life and working hard to achieve those goals."

"Selflessness" was the unequivocal principle noted by John G. He called it "a major component of maturity and so important to the fabric of our families and communities. It is also frequently elusive." Very well put!

Steve said, "I'm more humble than I used to be and less judgmental. Generally, I wish the best for others. My kids are the most important people in my life; they represent my best success."

Vincent, a 24-year-old pilot, offered this: "In my life, I try to respect others, live with an open mind, and do what I can to ensure the happiness of those around me. When I look in the mirror, I see a man who can look himself squarely in the eye and be proud of everyday."

Dan, a 53-year-old judicial consultant said. "I think the term 'self-image' may be a little misleading. I think that 80 to 90 percent of our self-image comes from how we are raised and the values put forth by family, friends and relatives. This includes love and acceptance for what we are and then recognition and support for what we do."

Colin, a 21-year-old theater manager, remarked, "I'm not willing to compromise the values I was raised to believe in—like honor and integrity—just to accommodate my own advancement. I'd rather rely on hard work and persistence."

"When I look in the mirror," Paul, our fireman, told me, "I see a vertically challenged gentleman who has a great smile, who loves his wife and son, and who can't wait to go to work in the morning." You have to like that!

Our 81-year-old, Max, offered this nugget of wisdom: "Character is the operative word here. Unfortunately, we are not born with it, so that each of us is left to develop it in his own way."

Here's the challenge that every great guy seems willing to accept.

⁂

QUESTION THREE: Social Skills and Common Courtesy. *How important are good manners to you now? Do you generally stand when a woman approaches your table? Do you wait for everyone to be seated before eating? Are you a man who* *still believes that opening a door for a lady is the proper thing to do?*

The answers are fascinating.

Mark said, “Good manners show that you are aware that others exist; it sends a signal that you’re paying attention. It’s like walking down the sidewalk and someone passes you going the other way; there’s not another soul around for blocks. Why would you not acknowledge their existence?” How true!

In Dan’s eyes, “Manners are the ‘grease’ that allows people in the world to find common ground.” He says, “Manners provide space and ‘rules’ to allow us to interact in ways that we can accept. The specific rituals that are labeled as ‘manners’ change with culture, but they do exist. The key in any case is respect. The guidepost for me is what might be called the ‘Hippocratic Oath of Manners’: In all situations, show no disrespect.” Wouldn’t it be great if the entire world took such an oath? Think of it.

Max had a similar view. “Civility is more than mere protocol. It serves to grease the wheels in our dealings with each other. Courtesy toward our women seems to me to be a pretty good place to start.”

John N., a spry 60-year-old actor, stressed the importance of such simple things as opening a door for a lady and rising when she approaches the table “I’m rather old-fashioned that way.” Old-fashioned or timely, it’s a nice thing for a lady to hear.

David said, “I think good manners are important, whether it’s opening a door for someone or waiting until everyone receives their food before beginning to eat. More importantly, however, I believe that rudeness is never appropriate.”

"Good manners are always appropriate. Holding a door open for someone is a thoughtful act," John G. observed. "It shows that you're aware of their imminent needs, big or small."

Bruce saw it this way: "Good manners are important, especially if practiced consciously."

Keith said, "Doing the little things is the most effective way of gaining respect. I once read that, 'A man's character is his fate,' and I believe it."

There it is. Character is timeless. It's also a conscious choice.

QUESTION FOUR: Confrontation. *Short of walking away, how do you deal with someone who is rude and disrespectful in his or her general behavior? In a social setting? In the course of business? When his or her behavior is directed at someone important to you?*

"Diplomacy is almost always the best way to disarm the disingenuous and disrespectful person," Steve told me. "My goal with people like that is to get what I need from them, to make it seem like it was their idea, and then move on."

Rick, the schoolteacher in our group offered these pearls of wisdom. "It's important to understand," he said, "that rude and disrespectful people are unpredictable, therefore potentially volatile and even dangerous. In a social setting, attempts to deflect—like changing the subject or saying something benign or funny—can be useful. At work, I confront only to resolve an issue, not for retribution. In either case, I examine my actions to see if I have provoked."

David expressed what a lot of us feel in these situations. "Unfortunately, I do not respond well to rudeness, and I'm prone to confront someone without regard to the setting. My challenge is to find a more appropriate and effective solution. Even in a professional setting, there is never an excuse for rudeness."

Paul also related what many of us feel: "When I'm forced to deal with someone who is rude or disrespectful toward me, I generally let it roll off my back. They're not worth my time." In a business setting, he said, "I would carefully weigh my options before acting. In business, you have to look at the long-term consequences of your responses and remember that it's not personal."

Dan had this perspective: "Rudeness is dealt with in degrees. Unintentional rudeness elicits a different response than the intentional. The continuum of responses goes from understanding and probing for more understanding to ignoring the situation and, finally, to leaving. But the truth is, confrontation is seldom a successful strategy in dealing with rudeness."

Our pilot made an interesting point: "I think it's important to point out your displeasure for a person's disrespectfulness. They should know your opinion."

Colin said, "Rudeness suggests a lack of security. I'd rather take such an incident and learn from it."

Max summed it up nicely. "Having the skill to 'smooth the waters' can be an advantage to a gentleman, who, by definition, is at ease in every kind of company."

QUESTION FIVE: Situation #1. *You're adrift at sea. Your vessel is sinking fast. There is only one space left on a lifeboat crowded with frightened people, including your family. It's come down to you and a young woman. Assume the lifeboat will capsize*

if you both attempt to get aboard. It's you or her. What do you do? And just as importantly, why do you do it?

Vincent gave this assessment: "Where you are in your life would play a major factor. As a single male, I would probably give her the spot. If, on the other hand, I had a wife and young kids, I would probably choose to stay and help my family. Hopefully, the woman would understand this."

David, the doctor in our group, responded, "I believe that if I had to choose between my life and someone else's, I would choose my own. Self-preservation is an instinct and not usually the product of a rational or logical thought." You have to appreciate David's candor.

Steve offered a different view. "I would hope I'd be a big enough person to offer that last spot to the young woman. After all, to sacrifice your own life for another is the ultimate in heroism. Furthermore, I don't think I could look myself in the mirror if I allowed her to die."

Bill, our contractor, stated it this way: "There are truly too many factors to do much more than guess, but I can say that my decision would depend far more on the young woman's character than her gender."

"I hope that I would give my space to the young woman and then try like hell to save myself in some other way," our option trader chimed in.

Our forensic investigator, a gentleman in his early 50s, saw the dilemma this way: "At my age, I'd like to think that I'd give up the spot, but I don't know for sure. The desire to be safe and with my family would likely be overwhelming." Even the most die-hard great guys would surely feel much the same.

Our fireman noted the difference between the "movie"

answer and the "reality" answer by saying, "In reality, yes, you let her get on the boat. But I'll be damned if I wouldn't try to find something else to keep me afloat until we were rescued, if for no other reason than my family."

Our schoolteacher Rick said, "Because she is young, I would encourage her to go since she has a lot of life to live. Then, I would hustle an alternative flotation device, dive overboard, and hang close to the lifeboat. The captain can go down with the boat."

⁂

QUESTION SIX: Outlook. *What is MOST important to you? Is it your job, your place in the community, the well-being of your family, or the state of your health? Why?*

We found the answers hopeful and refreshing.

Dan offered a more global view "A rich life is a matter of balance. Having a sense that you are part of a larger family and community; having work that is intellectually challenging; and having good health—these things are all integrally important to me."

John G. pointed to his family's well-being first and foremost. "That is just far and away the most important to me. This is built-in; there's no accounting for it. We are part of something larger. A healthy, happy family makes that 'something' better."

John N. was even more pointed "My children; they mean everything."

While Vincent agreed that the well-being of his family was of utmost importance, he also noted, the equally significant task of "preparing for a family of my own."

David, on the other hand, offered an opposing view: "I

think that my physical and mental health are my most important assets. Without those, I am unable to help my family or do my job, both of which are extremely important to me."

It's interesting to note that both views add up to the respondents' desire to take care of the needs of others.

At 19, Keith observed this: "I was raised to be an individual, a very independent individual but, contrary to that line of thought, I believe the best way to judge my life is to look at my relationships with the people closest to me, especially my family."

"If I'm healthy in my mind, body and spirit, I can be a better father, brother and friend," Steve told us. "If I feel good about my relationships, including my relationship with myself, then I can do my job that much better. These all facilitate any contributions to the community."

That sums it up nicely, don't you think?

❧ ❧ ❧

QUESTION SEVEN: Advice. *If you could share one or two pieces of advice with a young man who is just setting out in this increasingly difficult world, what would they be?*

Bruce began with this far-reaching advice: "Be compassionate and responsible and recognize the importance of paradox, humor, and change in life."

Rick, a man who spends his days teaching 4th graders, said, "Be bold while being respectful. Be assertive and gentle at the same time. Love to experience the phenomenon of relationship, not self-indulgence. Remember, it's you who chooses the way you feel, so FEEL. Last, but not least, there's always room for a good beer."

Dan, a man who spends his days advising judicial systems adds, "Be persistent. Be focused. Have an appreciation for how you fit into the larger scheme of things (whether it be religion, politics, etc.). Trust in your own abilities and be respectful of others." There's that word "respectful" again.

It was interesting to hear John G.'s thoughts. "Have reasonable expectations, especially when it comes to your family. Work hard, have fun and keep the company of optimistic people. Pray a lot."

David, the physician in our group, had a similar view. "Always work hard. Hard work will get someone further than brains or luck. Second, avoid excessive use of alcohol and drugs."

Vincent contributed this sage but simple piece of advice: "Be yourself."

Thomas, an 80-year-old gardener, shared this: "Preparation is the key to life. You never know what surprises life might have in store for you, and you want to be ready when the surprise happens."

Mark's advice was this: "Listen to others; ask questions so you have something to listen to. Don't ever assume you've got all the answers. Nobody does. Everybody is ignorant about something, and everybody has something they can teach you."

Our youthful fireman was succinct in saying, "Never give up hope. Steady the course."

Our retiree offered what he called the "Common Law" in seeking the good life: "Rule 1: Do all you have agreed to do. Rule 2 : Do not encroach on other people or their property."

And finally, from the writer in our group comes this advice: "First and foremost, believe in yourself. Believe that you can rise above the turmoil of the world and create your own legacy."

In many ways, that is what all of our great guys are suggesting: Create a legacy that you will be proud to leave behind.

QUESTION EIGHT: Years Gone By. *Do you believe that men and their attitudes have changed since you were growing up?*

There was a general consensus among our group of great guys that they had, though not always for the better.

The writer expressed it this way: "There is less idealism than there was; I sincerely hope this doesn't lead to cynicism. I worry that position and money have too high a place in the priority paradigm. I do, however, like most of the young men I meet, and that is a good sign."

Mark seemed to be of two minds about the question: "Yes, some. I think it's more of a black-and-white world when it comes to men, but it's hard to say. Maybe in the old days guys had more ways of hiding their behavior at work and at play." If Mark is implying that men are becoming more open and perhaps more honest, then that is a trend we need to applaud as well as encourage.

Dan offered this: "The ritual of manners will change with time. However, the attitude that it takes to live successfully in society changes less quickly. We are social animals who want to be loved and to belong. Respecting ourselves and others are guideposts that have survived centuries and many different cultures."

Here's what Max and his 81 years of experience noted: "I don't believe the 'so-called' change in the status of women suggests any real justification for discontinuing the little acts of chivalry we men enjoy performing and that our women still appreciate."

Bill stated, "They have changed, but not quickly enough."

John G. was considerably less optimistic. "Yes, men's beliefs and attitudes have changed, as have women's. We seem more selfish in my view."

Our 80-year-old gardener agreed, "People are so much more ME oriented. It worries me."

Bruce offered a different view, saying men's attitudes were improved, especially toward women. "The days of Frank Sinatra and his pals patting a woman on the rear in public while calling her 'doll' are happily history."

The youthful view of our pilot suggested that the attitudes of men he has grown up with have remained constant. "But this is positive," he said, "since I always saw their attitudes as good to begin with."

The view of our doctor was equally positive. "I think that men are far more inclined to recognize women as equals, which is not something I learned from my father. His generation was different."

What these answers suggest is that it's not enough just to change; the change has to be positive, and it has to be conscious. It's a serious responsibility, and one the great guy seems willing to accept.

❧ ❧ ❧

QUESTION NINE: Situation #2. *A young man is dating a woman he likes a lot. He's interested in initiating a sexual relationship. How would you advise him to proceed? If she's resistant, how far should he go, or how much should he do to coax her on? If she prefers to wait, should he respect her wishes and continue to see her, or should he move on to someone new?*

Our great guy schoolteacher said, "I would talk to him about how sex influences a relationship. It makes it more complex, challenging and complicated, not a bad thing, mind you, but true. I would tell him that coaxing should be avoided. It is manipulative and self-serving. If she prefers to wait and he does not, both positions should be clearly expressed. That takes real communication and generates mutual respect."

Paul, one of the younger members of our group, said, "I still hold to the old-school traditions that say you should wait for marriage to have a sexual relationship with your significant other. It's a simple answer to a complex and sometimes mixed-signal guessing-game, which it shouldn't be."

Bruce emphasized, "A sexual relationship should arise naturally and mutually."

David had this advice: "If it's sex he's interested in, he should just be honest and say so. The next move is hers. If she's not interested, move on. Coaxing a woman in order to have sex is emotionally dishonest and will eventually hurt both parties."

"My advice is talking it over," our public school administrator said. "Make sure you're both on the same page. Yes, you should respect her wishes for a time. If she's holding out for marriage, however, that's a different story. Then, it might well be time to move on."

"The ability to build a strong bond should be based on many factors," our pilot noted, "not just one."

John G. added this: "Respect her wishes. If you feel she's the 'one,' then things will eventually work out in all respects."

Keith had this to say: "Confidence is one of the most important things in life, and if she's not comfortable with sex yet, he should not press it. It's not worth the risk of damaging the relationship over this issue."

We were amazed and impressed at how often honesty lay at the heart of the matter. For a great guy, it's a way of life.

❧ ❧ ❧

QUESTION TEN: Money. *Are you a man who generally insists on picking up the tab when you're out with a lady, or are you comfortable with her pitching in every once in a while? How important is it that you earn more money than the woman in your life?*

The purpose behind this question is to discover whether the long-held views of our fathers' generation have evolved with increasing "equality" for us women. How does a schoolteacher respond to this? Rick says, "I have no problem sharing costs or being with a woman who makes more money than I do. It's the nature of my profession."

John G., our 54-year-old forensic investigator, took this approach: "In a dating situation," he says, "I think it's still appropriate for the guy to pay. If she makes more money, that's great."

Bruce had a slightly difference slant. "I would prefer to earn more money than the woman in my life in order to make life easier for her."

Mark countered that view, remarking, "Splitting the tab is always fine although picking it up feels good." He says, "It's not at all important to earn more money than my wife."

David was more adamant. "I always pick up the tab on a

date. I frequently offer to pick up the tab whether my companion is male or female, although I don't argue if someone wants to share the tab. The hypothetical question of a woman making more money is tough if it's never happened to you; my view is that as long as I'm being paid a fair salary it doesn't matter what someone else is paid."

Steve, a writer by trade, said, "I like being able to take a lady out to dinner or a movie. On the other hand, it also makes me feel special when she offers to take me out, too. For me, it's not a man/woman issue as much as it is wanting to make your mate feel special. The earnings issue is a matter of ego, and men and women alike are susceptible to that dilemma. I'd like to be the bigger man and say for certain that it doesn't matter who earns more; I'd like to believe that we would be able to put the health of the relationship above finances, but that's often easier said than done."

Colin said, "I have to remember that it's not always in the best interest of the relationship to pay for everything. There's a give and take that adds value to the relationship and reinforces the fact that we're equals, and this applies to finances and money, too."

What these answers suggest is that a great guy continues to learn about himself and that he's willing to allow his relationships to grow and change. That makes him more human, which makes him more attractive.

QUESTION ELEVEN: Situation #3. *You take a job in a good friend's company. Things seem to be going well. A number of years later, he comes in to your office and fires you. He's polite*

about it, even apologetic, but he wants to make a change. You're shocked. How do you react? How would you expect it to affect your long-term relationship? Anticipate your behavior the next time you see him.

Let's see how some of our group responded to this. David replied, "This is where professional behavior is most important. I would trust that my friend is doing what he must do. This should not necessarily affect a strong friendship. My concern upon our next meeting would be for his well-being."

That shows tremendous courage as well as style, doesn't it?

Our fireman showed equal class. "Just like a marriage, communication and listening will play key roles in this situation, and our long-term relationship would depend on how it was handled. The job may have ended but, with a good friend, the friendship doesn't."

"If I understood the reason," Rick said, "I could accept the decision and continue to relate. If I questioned the validity of the decision, I would probably find myself thinking less of the individual and seeing less of him as well."

Similarly, Bruce added, "If my friend's reasons for firing me were sound, and if he were a man of honor, we could probably patch the friendship. If, after due consideration, I still felt blindsided, then I could be cordial with him but probably not close friends."

John G.'s reaction was a mixture of both the professional and the personal. "I would probably react the same as if it were the 'traditional' employer-employee relationship: shocked but without any option except to ask for a letter of recommendation and leave gracefully. Our long-term relationship would, I'm afraid, never be the same."

Mark came at the question with a different logic. "I would never have taken a job in a good friend's company to begin with. I have turned down jobs for that very reason." Advice worth considering, I think.

"I would expect a truly honest reason from a 'true' friend," Bill, our contractor, said. Not an unreasonable expectation from a gentleman. "And it would be virtually impossible for his explanation not to affect the future of the relationship, either positively or negatively."

Max summed it up for the group, "How about a look at the bright side? If the employer is a true friend, it's likely the firing will turn out to be a great favor in the long run."

What this suggests is that a great guy has the ability to take the long view even when the short-term consequences aren't that bright. In the end, it's often how you maneuver around the stumbling blocks of life.

⁂

QUESTION TWELVE: Situation #4. *You've been blackballed from a club you really wanted to join, and you find out that the culprit is a longtime friend. How does this affect your attitude toward this person? What do you say to him the next time you meet?*

John G. stated what many of us would feel: "Hard for my attitude toward the person not to be changed in a negative way."

Our doctor probably spoke for many of us as well, "I do not believe a true friend would do that to me."

Max was pragmatic. He said, "Clear the air! Ask your 'friend' what's going on."

Our writer had this view: "I would naturally be disappointed if this 'friend' didn't have enough respect for me to come to me beforehand and discuss the situation. The blackballing wouldn't bother me. His lack of respect would be disheartening."

How about the Groucho Marx approach from John N., our actor? He said, "I wouldn't want to be a member of any club that would have me as a member."

Vincent, our youthful pilot, took an introspective view, saying, "I would have to wonder how good a friend this really had been."

Bruce didn't quibble over the degree of the friendship. He said, "A friend, even a casual friend, never treats another friend in such a manner."

From our schoolteacher came this worldly view: "First of all, I would have to accept that the relationship was not what I thought it was. With this realization, I would no longer 'trust' this person as I once had." He added, "Sometimes actions more clearly define a relationship. Most important would be spending time analyzing why I misunderstood the true nature of the relationship."

Mature and intelligent! Use the situation as a means to grow. I heartily approve.

QUESTION THIRTEEN: Sex. *Birth control is a sensitive, vital issue. In a dating situation, should a man provide his own birth control or should he expect his partner to provide protection for herself? If the woman he's sleeping with becomes pregnant, how would you advise him to handle the situation? Would you expect his approach to the situation to be different if he loved the woman?*

Mark, a great guy who works in the area of public education, said, "Always be prepared. A gentleman should always be prepared to talk about all the consequences of any activity in which he's engaging." Sound advice!

Our doctor shared this piece of advice: "The birth control issue must be settled *before* having sex. It is absolutely the responsibility of both parties." As for the issue of pregnancy, he added, "Again, both parties share equal responsibility; love has nothing to do with it, unless, of course, they want to get married."

Bill came straight to the point, "A wise and willing male should always have protection on hand; if she has it covered, so much the better." He also cautioned, "Pregnancy alone is the wrong reason to marry."

Rick emphasized, "If pregnancy occurs, the couple should discuss and decide what to do together, with respect for the more powerful impact the pregnancy will have on the woman. The conversation must be open and honest and both individuals should take full responsibility for whatever direction is determined. If there is disagreement, both parties must work at understanding the other, and accept either compromise or resignation without resentment."

As we noted earlier, a great guy understands just how poisonous resentment can be in any relationship; he works overtime to avoid alienating the people in his life because he knows that resentment is one of the most difficult and damaging defense mechanisms to overcome.

"If you're a sexually active male, then there's nothing more foolish or irresponsible than not having a condom in your wallet," Colin said.

On the issue of pregnancy, 24-year-old Vincent said, "If

the woman he is seeing becomes pregnant, it is the true test of the man. He should be fully responsible for his role in that child's life. This may not entail marriage. But the couple must remember that they are bringing a new life into the world, and they should each play a role in that life."

Age clearly has no bearing on wisdom.

Though Bruce expressed his opposition to abortion in the case of an unexpected pregnancy, he said, "They need to make their own thoughtful decision. I would, however, advise against abortion in favor of adoption or raising the child himself or herself. If they are in love, I would urge them to raise the child together."

Paul expressed a sex-after-marriage viewpoint: "I feel a person can find other ways to 'satisfy' themselves, like having a fulfilling and meaningful relationship, and put the sexual side of the relationship on hold until you take your vows.'"

Here's what I think. While our fireman's answer might strike some of us as old-fashioned, others would consider it the new wave of thinking. In either case, a gentleman knows that abstinence is in no way related to being a man: It's a choice, and a great guy believes in making his own choices. And, if our panel of gentlemen is any indication, his choice, when it comes to the issue of birth control, is one of responsibility and respect, both for his lady and himself.

QUESTION FOURTEEN: More Advice. *Assume the parents of our great guys aren't particularly taken with the woman he is seeing. How would you advise him to handle the situation?*

From our esteemed 81-year-old came this: "A gentleman has to be direct; it's his challenge to find out what's bugging the parents. That will give a clue as to what to do."

From our fledgling 19-year-old we heard, "Family is extremely important in life, and nobody should have a prolonged disagreement with their parents. It's the task of both parties to work it out."

Our writer said, "My parents raised me to think for myself and to trust my instincts. If they have misgivings, they need to communicate them in a way that doesn't alienate their son. If they ultimately create a 'her-or-us' situation, then they aren't showing much respect for their son. The key here is communication and honesty. It's about conserving relationships, not jeopardizing them, and the responsibility for that lies with both the parents and the son. Would I ask my son to give up a love interest because I wasn't overly excited about her? No."

John N., our youthful 60-year-old actor, said with complete sincerity, "As hard as it may be, our young man should take their advice." John's contention is that parents have a way of seeing down the road when the relationship takes on its long-term dynamics when sex and romance take a backseat to things like home and family and career.

Like John N., Bruce would advise our great guys not only to talk in earnest with his parents about their disapproval, but also "to seriously consider their opinion."

Bill felt that it was wise for our young man to find out the "why" affecting his parents and then to try to view his woman through their eyes. Sound advice. But in the end, he said, "Follow your own heart."

Twenty-one-year old Paul suggested interaction. He said,

"I would tell him to seek different opportunities to bring everyone together and share a variety of experiences. Hopefully this will help his parents see the many 'sides' of his woman."

Vincent went a step further, making it clear that both parties have a responsibility here. He said, "Our gentleman should strive to show his parents the positive reasons why he is seeing this woman. He should try to make them aware of the good in her. The parents, for their part, should not be too quick to judge and in time will hopefully discover the same positive qualities their son sees in her."

While our doctor advised our young man to make an effort "to determine the cause of his parents' feelings," he also said, "Ultimately it's none of their business. Many happy marriages exist despite parents' misgivings."

❧ ❧ ❧

QUESTION FIFTEEN: Situation #5. *If you discovered that the woman you were dating had a drinking or drug problem, how would you react?*

This is not an easy question. The great group of guys we've been describing is a man who goes out of his way to see to the needs of others and who most often puts the best interest of our planet ahead of personal gain. Yet, every man has to choose his battles. He has to understand his abilities and where those abilities are best placed. Let's hear how our group responded to this particular "battle."

John G., our forensic expert, offered an answer that required no elaboration. He said simply, "I'd move on."

Max offered a similar view, but with this explanation:

"Unless the gentleman craves the prospect of living on an emotional roller coaster, he should do the generous thing and leave the woman to one who does."

Vincent posed this youthful view: "I would think the woman might need time away from dating to deal with these serious problems. If this was someone I still wanted to be with, I would remain in her life as a friend and supporter."

Rick brought another element into the picture. He said, "I would have to insist she accept some type of positive intervention, or I would be forced to leave the relationship."

"I have been involved in such a situation, and it is tough," Bruce admitted. "If I were to relive the situation, I would tell her that she must seek counseling or I would be forced to end the romantic part of the relationship. If she did seek help, I would work with her for a reasonable time, probably a year. If she did not seek help, it is likely that I would have to end the relationship entirely." The voice of experience!

Steve said, "This is a problem that can be solved, but not easily and not without the firm commitment of the woman. And, if the woman is an alcoholic or an addict, the problem is lifelong. If I love this person, then I'm always willing to help her overcome the problem, but I would not be willing to allow the problem to rule our lives."

Our youthful student said, "The man should relish the opportunity to make a positive, long lasting impact on the life of someone close to him."

What about this view from David? "Simply confront the problem honestly and openly. She needs help. If he loves her, he will do everything to support her, except allowing her to continue the drinking or drugging."

We have talked about the characteristics that make a true great guy, and now we have heard from some live Mr. Real Deals in person. The truth is, these men live lives very much like our own. They live honestly. They make mistakes and learn from them. They see problems, and they turn their energies toward solving them. They don't walk over people; they lend a hand. They face their fears and try not to turn them into acts of destruction or turmoil. They act. They care. They love.

Her: "I grew up in Columbus, Ohio, and both of my parents were from there also. What about you?"

Him: "I really don't care to answer a bunch of questions."

Lesson: This man is a waste of time. He is not interested in sharing and it doesn't matter what the reasons are.

CHAPTER TEN

A WOMAN'S PERSPECTIVE

We need to set standards for ourselves. We need to set standards for the men in our lives.

As women, we take an interest in most everything. Whether it's politics or people, religion or nature, food or fashion, education or health, we want to be sponges, absorbing information, knowledge and insight. That's what makes the world go round. That's also what makes us fascinating and compelling individuals. We know that dismissing things out of hand or as unimportant is a surefire way of closing our minds, and we're nothing if not open-minded. I'm not suggesting we're experts in every area we take an interest in. It's the learning process that's fascinating.

We want a man who shares this diversity. We don't need to have all the same interests; it's more a matter of sharing the fascination. We should be able to grow from our mutual interest in each other's work, hobbies, avocations and dreams. Ladies, you can tell if a man is truly interested in you and your life by watching his eyes and his posture. Does he ask questions? Are his questions heartfelt? Is he dismissive?

"I don't ask the world. I just want him to be as interested in what I'm doing as I am in what he's doing. And it has to be genuine. He has to be the most important person in my life, and I have to be the most important in his. Otherwise, it's not a primary relationship."
—Amy, a 33-year-old business owner and single mom

❧ ❧ ❧

Know Thyself

This is something we can ask only of ourselves, but it's a trait that separates the great guy from the cad in a heartbeat. He's not afraid of knowing himself. Far from it, ladies!

One thing we can ask of the men in our lives is that they take the good along with the bad and run with it. This is a life philosophy in many ways. It's like looking in the mirror. We can't hide from what the mirror is telling us about the way we look. What we can do is accent our good features and make do with those that aren't so hot.

If we can put aside our fears, we can also discover a different kind of mirror that allows us to see the "real" you and "real" me. It's the mirror of our relationships: with our men, our friends and family, our colleagues at work, even the homeless guy on the street corner. It's our relationships with nature and God and the hidden corners of our own minds. That's the beauty of it.

Find a man who's not afraid to look into that mirror, and you're onto something. A guy who's not afraid to step up to the plate and take a hard look at the way he relates to the rest of the world is halfway to becoming Mr. Real Deal. Sure, he might not like everything he sees. Who does?

❧ ❧ ❧

> *"The most important thing in my life is following through. If I give my word, it's a promise. As a man, my word has to have impact. If people don't trust me to keep my word, then I'm not honoring our relationship."*
>
> —Keith, a 19-year-old student and emerging Great Guy

❧ ❧ ❧

"Lofty" Is Not Such a Bad Thing to Aim For

I'm referring here to a little thing called respect, and the awesome task of treating everyone with the same respect…and that is most certainly a lofty goal.

We can give respect because someone is in a position to advance our cause or because that someone deserves it. Ironically, the latter is so much easier. So in the end, the doorman at a hotel deserves the same courtesy as the business partner we're meeting inside the hotel.

Here's a simple test, one we can take or one we can give to the men in our lives.

Do you (they) treat children and young adults with the same attention as you (they) do the senior partner of a law firm or the senior citizen walking his dog in the park? How did you do? How'd your man do?

⁂

"We are social animals who want to be loved and to belong, and respecting ourselves and others are guideposts that have survived through the centuries and beyond cultures."

—Dan, a 53-year-old judicial consultant and longstanding great guy

⁂

It's a Hard, Cruel World Out There

It sure is. And there are plenty of times when it would be nice to know someone with all the answers. Someone who could tell us why the world is the way it is, or how we can rise above it all. Someone who could explain why people do what they do to each other. A politician or a religious leader. A teacher or a poet or a man on a mountain.

No way, girls. He or she doesn't exist.

The thing is, we probably don't want a guy who believes in one all-inspiring guru either. If we're looking for a barometer of the male psyche, try juxtaposing a man who's more interested in looking for answers against one who thinks he has the answers already. It's not much of a contest, is it? It doesn't matter whether he looks for inspiration from Gandhi or Bob Dylan—the point is whether or not he's willing to look. A man doesn't have to spend his free time reading Shakespeare or listening to CNN, but he sure as heck has to be willing to listen to our views if we do have an interest in Shakespeare and hear our opinions if we happen to be fans of CNN. You may read the *Rig Veda* one night and listen to a Colin Powell speech the next.

If we're inspired by something as simple as a falling leaf or the sound of a baby laughing, that doesn't necessarily mean that he's going to be moved by the same things, but it's worth watching how he responds to a conversation with a good friend or a comment from a learned colleague. No reaction at all is not a good sign, in my opinion.

When all is said and done, a great guy knows that the key is an open mind. It's not one book, and it's not one man, and it's not wishful thinking.

"Character is the important thing in building a positive image of ourselves."

—Mary, a 61-year-old attorney and wife of 40 years

It's Not the Money, Honey

It's not the easiest lesson to learn, but when all is said and done, money has no real power of its own.

That's not to say that we don't recognize that money has a necessary part in our lives; the trap is sprung when we come to see money, in and of itself, as the one force that drives our lives. Then, we start to judge the men we meet by their incomes or their automobiles. Nothing's wrong with wealth or fast cars—until we start seeing them as the solutions to our problems. They're not; they're tools.

There are lots of men out there who would trade love or friendship for money. A great guy isn't one of them. Is he willing to put his nose to the grindstone to earn a good salary or turn a profit? Darn right. Does he understand that hard work and long hours are at the heart of any successful endeavor? Count on it. Is he willing to sell his soul for a healthy paycheck or a quick retirement? No more than you and I are.

> *"The nice thing about money is that you have a choice whether to let it rule your life or not."*
> —Alice, a 43-year-old writer and divorcee

❧ ❧ ❧

The Difference Between Excellence and Perfection

You and I know that people aren't perfect. But we also understand it's our flaws and imperfections that make us unique and special.

Try applying that to the man in your life the next time he leaves the toilet seat up or makes one of his outrageous comments.

Excellence, on the other hand, defies definition. Why? Because what I see as common and ordinary might just strike you as extraordinary. It could be a fine wine or a painting on a wall. It could be the smell of a spring day or an unexpected smile. It could be a stock option, a set of blueprints, or an idea written on the back of a cocktail napkin.

Look for a man who strives for excellence without confusing it with perfection, a man who's ambitious without being obsessive, and a man who's organized without being compulsive, and you may have just hooked yourself a great guy.

❧ ❧ ❧

"When I look in the mirror, I see a man who is sometimes selfish and stubborn, a man who can on occasion be a pain in the ass, but also a guy who is without question a good and loving father, a loyal husband and friend, and a man who values honesty and integrity as much as he does tolerance and compassion."

—Bruce, a 54-year-old futures trader and a forthright great guy

❧ ❧ ❧

It's Not a Gender Thing, It's Not a Race Thing, and It's Not a Religion Thing. It's a People Thing.

We respect individuality. We appreciate freethinking and diversity. We know, however, that individuality and diversity are meant to enhance relationships and improve things like productivity and creativity, not drive a wedge between people. Now the question is, Does he know this?

"I'm amazed at how much emphasis we put on the 'race' thing. It's such a fallacy. If we're all the same biologically, then there can only be one race, and that's the human race. Think of how much turmoil we could avoid if we could just get that message across."

—Colin, a 21-year-old theater manager and up-and-coming great guy

When All Is Said and Done, the Key to This Life Adventure Is Love

You and I realize that love—real love—comes about only when there are no so-called "barriers" between us and our significant others.

This is crucial in a relationship. It's not a place for compromise or "just settling."

Our aim is to accept other people for who they are, not what they are, and a man who thinks otherwise is not about to qualify as a great guy.

Our goal is to accept other people without letting our prejudices get in the way.

Taking a risk.

Putting ourselves on the line.

Harder yet is giving affection without expecting anything in return; letting ourselves in for some rejection.

We know that love isn't the easiest route to take—it's just the most worthwhile. Can we insist upon that from the men in our lives? Absolutely.

"When it comes time for me to share a few words of wisdom with my son when he sets out in the world, I think I'll tell him that he can be daring and still be respectful; he can assert himself and still be kind; he can experience love and passion without being self-indulgent."

—Sharon, a 29-year-old schoolteacher, wife and mother

THE GREAT GUY QUESTIONNAIRE FOR MEN ONLY

Challenge him. See how he responds.

We invite you to challenge the man in your life with the Great Guy questionnaire below. There are no right or wrong answers, only a chance for him to get to know himself a little better. If he's daring enough, he won't be afraid to share the results with you and hear what you have to say.

Personal History

Who was most influential in teaching you the important lessons in life? For example, right versus wrong, actions have consequences, etc. Is there an example you can cite?

Self-image

What are you most proud of in your life? For example, would it be your parenting skills or your business acumen, your community service or your commitment to family? Please explain.

Social Skills and Common Courtesy

Are good manners important to you? For example, do you make it a point of opening doors for women or greeting your guests with a cup of coffee or glass of wine?

Confrontation

Short of walking away, how do you handle someone who is disrespectful or rude to you, whether it's a co-worker, a friend or a family member?

Outlook

What is MOST important to you? Is it your job, your place in the community, the well-being of your family, or the state of your health? Why?

Money

In a dating situation, are you a man who generally insists on picking up the tab, or are you comfortable with her pitching in occasionally? Are there exceptions? What effect does this have on the relationship?

Sex

Should a man provide his own birth control or should he expect his partner to provide protection for herself? Please explain.

Advice

If you could share one or two pieces of advice with a young gentleman who is just setting out in this increasingly difficult world, what would they be?

Situation #1

A young man is in a dating situation with a lady he likes a lot. He wants to initiate a sexual relationship. How should he proceed? If she's resistant, how far should he go to coax her on? If she prefers to wait, should he respect her wishes or should he move on to someone new? Please explain.

Situation #2

You take a job working for a good friend. All indications suggest that you're doing a good job. Several years later, he fires you. He's polite about it, but he wants to make a change. You're shocked. How do you react? How would it impact your long-term relationship? Anticipate your behavior the next time you see him.

Situation #3

A man is sexually involved with a woman he likes but does not love. She becomes pregnant and insists on having the child. How would you advise him to proceed? How would your advice differ if he were your son?

Situation #4

A man is in love with a woman his parents don't like. How should he proceed?

Situation #5

You discover that the woman you're in love with has a drinking or drug problem. How do you proceed?

Her: “Tell me all about yourself. Where did you grow up? Where did you go to school? Do you have a girlfriend?”

Him: (Thinking to himself) “Oh, man, I have no interest in either her or these questions.”

Lesson: Make sure you ask a lot of questions right off the bat. If a man will not answer you honestly and completely, there is something wrong, and it’s bye-bye, honey!

CHAPTER ELEVEN
RAISING THE LITTLE DEVILS

There's no definitive handbook for raising a great guy in the 21st century. You can search the child psychology shelves in your local bookstore until you're exhausted and still come up empty-handed.

In all fairness, boys today often get a bad rap. Do they deserve it? Sometimes they do. Sometimes not.

It's true that boys are labeled with "learning disabilities" and "emotional problems" far more often than girls. It's true that they commit more violent acts than the opposite sex. They commit suicide at a far greater rate. The majority of our prisons are filled with men, not women. And for a good number of those women who do find themselves behind bars, there's often an abusive man in the picture somewhere.

So, how do we as parents steer our young men along the gentleman's path that we have described here?

It's probably wise to admit, first and foremost, that whoever told us, "No one said it would be easy" could very easily have been referring to the task of raising a great guy. Still, I would like to offer my own personal views on the subject of raising a young man.

IT'S NEVER TOO EARLY

Today, the messages of respect we share with our young men need to start early.

And by early, I am talking about the toddler level. Treat the girls on the playground with respect. Treat your sisters with respect. Treat the women in your life with respect. Treat the man from across the tracks with respect. Treat yourself with respect.

When your young man uses bully tactics, unnecessary force, or just brute strength to get his way with the little girl he's playing with in the sandbox, watch out. He needs to know that very moment that such behavior won't be tolerated. Run over, pick him up and remove him from the scene. Look him square in the eye. Tell him you expect him to be a "gentle giant," and make certain he knows that a gentle giant doesn't misuse his strength.

Start early! The later it gets, the harder it gets. He needs to know the rules long before you pack him off to kindergarten:

Don't slide into the water fountain.

Don't pull Susie's hair.

Don't grab at lunchtime.

Don't fight at recess.

Watch to see who's at the bottom of the slide.

Don't do this. Watch out for that.

There are a thousand dos and just as many don'ts. It's a jungle out there, and I am NOT kidding. Being a kid can still be fun, but there's NO TOLERANCE for the rough guy. Knowing the difference is the key.

THE OLD STEREOTYPES DIE HARD

For better or worse, there has not been a serious revision in the attitudes we hold toward the rearing of boys.

The traditional 19th-century theories continue to hold fast:

Boys should not whine.

Boys should not cry.

If they do cry, they'll sure as heck be bullied and taunted.

If they bully, they might just get caught.

If they get caught, they shouldn't complain.

Under no circumstances should they "tell" on the guy who betrayed them.

It's hell for the boy who gets off on the wrong track. Boys are silent sufferers, which means it's harder to get through to them. Which means it's harder to help them.

"Who punched you?" you ask.

If he tells, he knows you'll call the school. If you call the school, the other kids will know he's weak. What to do? If the school has mentors or teachers who know their stuff, they may be able to take the bully and his victim aside and reconcile issues on a one-on-one basis. Otherwise, you may be forced to intervene.

WHAT'S THE PLAN?

Start by sharing your day, your week, your plan.

Men are instinctive planners. Boys are, too. They need a plan. Give them one.

In raising a boy to be a man, preparation is key. Let him know well in advance about all the important events that are happening in his life. If it's the first day of school, talk to your little guy. Tell him how he's probably going to feel. Tell how you felt your first day of school. If you think you can't remember that far back, just give it a try. It's incredible how emotional events carve such powerful memories into the mind.

Discuss anger and fear at an early age so your young man can identify these remarkably strong male emotions. If he is not surprised by emotion, he can deal with it better. It's a tremendous gift. Whatever you do, don't make your boy feel ashamed for feelings that come so naturally to him. If there is no man around to share these kinds of feelings with your son, find one you trust.

Preparation is the key to getting your young man through his first birthday party, his first day of school, even his first sleepover. Preparation is also the key to getting him through drastic life changes, such as a death in the family or a divorce.

❧ ❧ ❧

THE SETTING IS IMPORTANT

While planning is important, so is your child's placement in a healthy, safe environment.

Whether it's his day-care setting or his preschool, his Boy Scout troop or his summer camp, the community settings you choose for your little devil are bound to have long-term ramifications. Make your choices accordingly.

Make sure you're familiar with the teachers who will be charged with bringing the messages of the world to your son. Have an idea of who the students sitting next to him in class are. Get to know their parents.

If your child is in an environment where he is viewed as a problem, you will have a problem child. If your child is viewed as a leader, he will lead. If your child is viewed as a delinquent, you will have a delinquent on your hands.

How exactly do your child's teachers perceive him? Ask them straight-out during those parent-teacher conferences that we all dread. How do the administrators at his school perceive him? Go right into their offices and ask them. If your child is perceived in a negative light, you should think seriously about moving him to another, more positive academic environment. Don't hesitate. If you must wait until the end of the year for a school change, make sure your home environment is supportive and caring. If you cannot afford a private school, you might even consider homeschooling. There is a whole world on the Internet of other home-schoolers. There is a *Home School Magazine*. Well-designed home school curricula make the process far simpler than you might imagine. And don't forget charter schools and religious schools. Explore your options.

Join a church, a sports group or the Boy Scouts to help your fledgling gentleman make friends outside of school.

Remember what Jackie Kennedy Onassis said: "If you fail with your kids, nothing else really matters."

BAD MOON RISING

Make yourself aware of the telltale signs that your child is in trouble. And don't ignore them.

Your child will let you know if his school environment is painful for him:

He'll be tired.

He won't want to go to school.

He'll have a headache.

He'll hide his homework.

You'll get a call from the school itself.

After you have found out what the school thinks the problem is, decide for yourself. Then consider your options. Do your research. Ask questions. Talk to people. Use the Internet. Use your summers to plan trips that are both educational and fun. Create experiences that allow your son to figure out what he enjoys and what his interests are. You'll know when he knows, and then you can encourage his pursuit of those interests.

Use the outdoors to get close to your child. Take him camping. Allow him to feel strong. Teach him to feel good about himself. If he's struggling in school or having trouble making friends, send him to an outdoor program such as SOAR (Success

Oriented Achievement Realized) where he can meet other kids who are struggling. He won't feel so alone or isolated.

If your son's school reports continuous fidgeting and/or hyperactivity, you may need to see a doctor, and you may need to consider the use of medication. Don't be afraid of terms like ADD (Attention Deficit Disorder) and ADHD (Attention Deficit Hyperactivity Disorder) or even BiPolar Syndrome. These conditions are not psychological jail sentences. Millions of Americans have been diagnosed with these disorders, and most of them are doing fine. Do your research about these various disorders and the medicines that are being used to treat them. Access the Internet. Make sure your doctor is aware of your concerns and your questions. If, in the end, your doctor recommends some type of medication, consider it strongly. Millions of kids have been helped by medication in combating these disorders, and it might help your kid, too.

LAUGH EVEN WHEN IT HURTS

Whatever you do, never lose your sense of humor with your child.

Most boys are still in diapers when they begin to appreciate humor. As a parent, it's a tool that should be used early and often. It can deflect anger, balance frustration, and short-circuit bad behavior.

I will never forget the time my son threw a bowl of Raisin Bran right in my face. Talk about a shocker! I could have responded a dozen different ways. I chose humor. "So we would prefer Corn Flakes today?" I said calmly, trying to make light of it.

Later, we were horrified to discover our son, now 14 and a computer junkie, busily clicking his way from one pornographic Web site to another. My husband, who always looks for the light at the end of every tunnel, asked, "Do you think he's just studying to be a gynecologist?"

Don't forget that all things do eventually pass, and those that seem traumatic today will strike you as less traumatic tomorrow. I encourage you to look at the BIG PICTURE.

If your child is hyperactive or different in some organic way, it is also important to maintain perspective. A book I highly recommend is Dr. Edward M. Hallowell's *Driven to Distraction*. Dr. Hallowell uses the lighter side of his own ADHD (Attention Deficit Hyperactivity Disorder) as an effective means of advising parents how to handle their children's differences.

❧ ❧ ❧

THE HIGH ROAD

Praise, praise, praise! Then set some limits. Then establish some boundaries.

Whether the little devil in your care is difficult or not, the same rules apply in raising your child to be a great guy. He needs praise and lots of it. Whether he's helping Mom carry in the groceries or raking leaves in the backyard, he should be praised. And there's no better model for this good behavior than his dad. Get the two of them involved in helping out in the kitchen or doing some of those outdoor chores. What better time to praise your son for his efforts? When the young man in your life uses a kind voice with you or his dad or his siblings, even with the family pet, his good behavior should be recognized. When he doesn't, he should be made aware of his negative behavior as well.

If your young man needs the occasional reminder to keep him on task—and we all do—use a voice that will serve as a model for him. If you rely on sarcasm, he'll rely on it, too. If you rely on cynicism or rebuke, so will he. If you scream, he'll scream back.

Post rules so there's no misunderstanding about what you expect. Plan regular family meetings and give your young man an important role. Allow him to keep the meeting log. Let him call the meeting to order. Let him list all the good things each family member has been up to that week.

I like the way Jane Nelson put it when she said, "Where did we ever get the crazy idea that in order to make children do better, first we have to make them feel worse? Think of the last time you felt humiliated or treated unfairly. Did you feel like cooperating or doing better?"

MAMA'S BOY

Young gentlemen need their moms. There isn't a boy who doesn't.

Boys love their mothers. It doesn't matter whether they're raised on a farm or in the big city. It doesn't matter whether they have a dozen siblings or none at all. And I believe that boys are separated from their mothers emotionally at too young an age. If your young man wants a kiss, throw your arms around him. If he wants to wrestle, get down on the floor and wrestle. Remember to spend quality time every week with your boy and give him your undivided attention. If he wants to hang out with you every now and then or just sit and talk for a few minutes, don't put him off. He needs this connection. There's no substitute for it.

If a young man does not feel connected to his mom, I believe he will grow angry and bitter. And there's no age limit to this connection. Whether he's a toddler or a young adolescent, don't worry that he will be a sissy. These stereotypes have hurt our men. Let him spend the night on the floor near you if that's what he needs. Let him hold your hand. Let him cry or be afraid. Don't worry about what other people think.

THE PATH LESS TRAVELED

Don't for one second believe the phrase "Boys will be boys."

Boys don't really have to fit the stereotype of other boys. This is a myth just waiting to be broken. Boys come in all shapes and sizes. Some are artistic. Some are athletic. Some climb rocks. Some do not. You'll know who your young man is if you nurture his talents. This is the secret to raising a great guy.

Boys need heaps of love, just as girls do. Remember never to make him feel ashamed of who he really is. If you do, he'll be angry for the rest of his life.

Also remember to keep your own angry hands off your boy. If you strike him, he'll end up striking his own wife or kids. If you feel like striking him, leave the room. Get in the car. Listen to the radio until you cool off. If you DO strike him, apologize and tell him you are a human being who lost control.

Let him know you made a terrible, stupid, but very human mistake, hopefully a mistake that will never happen again.

DO AS I DO

Model good behavior, and your little devil will follow suit. It's guaranteed.

Your young man is watching you, even when you think he's not. He is observing how you treat people. He's listening to the tone of your voice. He is watching how you carry yourself.

Show him how to act by acting right.

Speak kindly to him. Greet him and other members of your family properly when they enter a room. When you leave, tell him when you'll be back, just as you would your husband or wife or a buddy. Don't speak rudely or loudly when you're on the telephone. The best way to teach a great guy-in-the-making common courtesy is to show him common courtesy in action—not as a part-time venture, but as a way of life.

Treat people of all stations in life kindly. He'll get the picture.

If you don't like when people get tattoos or wear earrings, talk about it. He may still get a tattoo or pierce an ear, but at least he's aware of your feelings. Tell him when he is 10, 11, 12 and 13 about how you feel about drug use or smoking. You can never start discussing this subject too early. Describe what happens to people who abuse drugs. Use a friend as an example if you have one. He'll be listening.

It is your job to teach. You are the teacher here.

He is yours, and he knows it.

TAKING THE PLUNGE

Young gentlemen learn by doing! It's a fact.

Men are vastly different from women in one unique respect. They seem to learn best by getting their hands dirty. Once they jump in, the wheels begin to turn.

If you want to talk to your son about something important, take him out to the golf course or break out your baseball mitts. Use the time to talk to him about whatever it is that's on your mind. While you're out hiking, tell him you're worried about his new friends. Express your concerns about the girl he's seeing while the two of you are mountain biking or fishing. He may not act like he is listening, but he is.

When you're in the car together, talk. It's the perfect time to get his attention. Let him talk. When he does, listen. If birth control or sex is an issue, relay your message by telling him a story about someone you knew who got a girl pregnant. There is a good reason why the Bible uses stories and proverbs to get Jesus' messages across. Nobody likes to be lectured. Everybody loves a good story. If it helps, see a movie with a message. Share a poem or the lyrics to a favorite song. Use your imagination.

You'll want to know about his friends, his hobbies and his whereabouts. It's part of your role as parent. He'll ask for privacy, and to some extent, you'll want to comply. Still, when all is said and done, you'll need to keep tabs on your child. It is your home, and he needs to abide by the "house rules" so long as he is under your roof. That's only fair. He'll do the same when he's a parent.

❧ ❧ ❧

WHEN ALL IS SAID AND DONE

Act with honor, and he'll mirror that behavior as he grows.

Approach life with a sense of humility, and he will begin to understand his place in the world.

Strive for integrity, and he'll stand a little taller in the face of adversity.

The last step after you've modeled your best behavior and done your best to open the lines of communication is to let your little devil know just how much you care. I'm not talking about his performance as much as I am his happiness. Let him know from Day 1 just how proud you are of him, and for no other reason than for who he is. Say "I love you" and mean it.

If you do it right from the very beginning, you'll wake up one day and the young boy sitting across from you at the breakfast table will be an up-and-coming great guy, all thanks to you.

SECRETS FROM THE AUTHOR

It's really hard to meet the right man. There is no question about that. It helps to be raised by the right father.

Most of us are not that lucky.

Some of us have to learn the hard way.

We have to learn to respect ourselves and take care of ourselves before we are really able to go find a wonderful partner.

Some of us end up hurting ourselves because we lack respect for ourselves. We put knives to our arms. We put markings on our bodies that must be removed at great expense and pain later. We starve ourselves.

It helps to know what you are looking for.

It helps to look for a man who respects himself and the planet he lives on.

You've heard a lot about that in my book.

I believe you have to look for a kind man.

Forget about Mr. Macho.

Watch how your man drives and speaks to waiters and handles everyday activities.

And if you love the man you are with and need to change him—you can.

You need to teach him how to be the man you want.

There's a whole history here to draw from.

Start asking questions and getting answers now.

Getting Started
The Code of a Great Guy

Committing yourself to the code of a great guy is much like mastering the art of being a great driver. It's easy in some respects and hard in others. The mechanics are easy. The nuances require attention and repetition. You learn to drive with one eye on the rearview mirror and the other on the side mirrors. You learn to drive defensively. You never let your emotions get in the way. Quite a feat, but it's well worth it.

We all expect our young men to take their places behind the wheel of a car at some point. It's a rite of passage. It's the American way. We should be placing the same expectation on acquiring basic social skills, the nuts and bolts of common courtesy, and a code of ethics and behavior. Committing ourselves to the code of a great guy should be part of the American way. Take the pledge. Get started today.

Pledge: I am a great guy. I commit myself to a life of self-respect. I place my honor and my integrity above all else. I will strive to overcome my natural-born insecurities. I will dedicate myself to building a legacy my kids will be proud to acknowledge and hopefully even follow.

My Commitment to the Public at Large

I will make it my goal to try to find the best in others.

I will approach the world with an open mind.

I will be careful about leveling criticism at others, whether it is warranted or not.

I will be especially kind and respectful to those in service positions. People who work at such places as restaurants, gas stations and banks deserve my humor, respect and kindness. I will not insult or belittle them.

My Commitment to My Coworkers

I will respect my coworkers regardless of their abilities or their positions.

I will remember especially to treat my female coworkers with uncommon respect. I will never verbally or physically abuse them, nor will I make unwarranted sexual references or gestures toward them.

I will offer a handshake to any and all who enter my office.

I will do my best never to "burn bridges."

My Commitment to My Immediate Family

I will strive for tolerance in dealing with my parents, my wife and my children.

I will never raise a hand to them.

I will be especially attentive and kind to my family because they represent my name and my legacy, but mostly because I love them.

My Commitment to My Mother and Father

I will respect my mother and father and speak well of them even in times of disagreement or discord.

I will keep an open line of communication with them.

I will allow them the freedom to know their grandkids and to spoil them the way they see fit.

My Commitment to My Wife and Partner

I will show my children how to treat a woman by respecting their mother.

I will respect her individuality and support her goals.

I will reserve sexual advances and sexual references toward her to private encounters.

I will do the simple things, like opening doors for her, complimenting her appearance, and offering a helping hand around the house.

I will always greet her when I enter a room, and I will always give notice when I'm leaving our home.

Should my wife and I go our separate ways, I will continue to respect her to the best of my ability.

My Commitment to My Children

I will teach my children by setting the best example possible, both in my actions and my words.

I will tell them each and every day how special they are.

I will teach them the value of self-respect and self-improvement.

I will teach them to stand up for what they believe in.

I will teach my children to love God as I know him.

My Commitment to My Children and the Ways of the World

I will teach my children how to greet adults by LOOKING THEM STRAIGHT IN THE EYE.

I will teach them the value of a firm handshake.

I will teach them the importance of kindness and respect towards their family and others.

I will teach them to lose without whimpering and to win without bragging.

I will teach them the value of good manners, whether it's standing when an adult approaches their table or waiting for everyone to be seated before they eat.

I will explain to my children that when they are in a group it is a courtesy to introduce strangers to one another. I will teach them to respect their elders by introducing them first.

I will explain to my children the importance of dressing appropriately for special events.

I will tell them never to lie about their background, but rather to speak with pride and honesty about it.

I will tell my children that they should feel free to dine

with all people regardless of their station in life, and that even presidents don't generally know which salad fork to use at a formal dinner.

I will use appropriate language in the company of my kids.

My Commitment to My Children and the Matter of Drugs and Alcohol

I will talk freely and openly with my children about drugs and alcohol.

I will paint a true picture of how drugs and alcohol affect our behavior.

I will lead by example.

Knowing that an active mind and body are less likely to be drawn to drugs and alcohol, I will encourage my kids to pursue their interests in the arts, in sports, in the great outdoors, or in whatever it is that moves them.

My Commitment to School and Learning

I will encourage my children in school because I know an educated mind has the best chance of success in our world today.

I will explain that learning is a humbling and awesome thing and that the more you learn, the more you will find there is to learn.

If the environment at my son's or daughter's school proves to be unhealthy, dangerous or detrimental to them in any way, I will seek to find an alternative schooling solution.

I will encourage my children to find their passion—cars,

rock climbing, birds, theater, painting, photography, computers, engines—whatever makes them want to live and learn.

My Commitment to the Earth

I will teach my children to be gentle with the Earth and to love the creatures in it.

I will make certain the children understand that the Earth is man's legacy and inheritance, and that it is our responsibility to respect it.

I will teach them to look at the Earth with humility. I will explain that the Earth and its resources were not put here for us to misuse and squander.

I will explain that while most hunters and fishermen love their sports, they also desire to preserve the land and to maintain the animal population they pursue.

My Commitment to Myself

I will put respect above possessions.

I will put my legacy and the well-being of our planet above the status of my stock portfolio.

I will look for solutions, not excuses.

I will view people with hope, not despair.

I will strive for tolerance.

I will speak out in the face of injustice no matter what the consequences.

Every day I will try to make one life a little easier.